1-MINUTE

HABITS

OPTIMISE YOUR BRAIN,

FORM ANY HABIT,

AND LIVE A FULFILLED LIFE

RAGHIB AHMED

Copyright and Disclaimer

Contents

Part 2: HOW

Preface

The amount of times I've struggled with achieving goals and resolutions in the past is too many to count. It seemed like there was a never-ending conflict between my long-term interests and my short-term interests. Unfortunately, the latter would usually come out on top at the expense of the former. I constantly struggled with temptations, distractions, procrastination, and a lack of motivation – all of which pushed me towards the path of least resistance and taking the easy way out. The outlook on achieving what I wanted looked bleaker and bleaker. If you have ever struggled with any of these things, then this book is for you.

It's interesting that it is the path of least resistance which makes us falter. The lack of 'resistance' makes this path much more desirable, which is why we are tempted to go down it so often. But this path usually contains the things that don't coincide with our goals. It contains things that may feel good now, but make us worse off tomorrow. If it's the path of least resistance that we constantly seem to cling onto, why don't we apply that to our goals? Doesn't it make complete sense rationally, to make the path of our goals the path of least resistance? The typical approach when achieving things is to see our goals as some extremely difficult task that is way out of our reach - so the only way to achieve it is to go all in. But as I, and so many of us, can vouch for, this approach doesn't always work.

This is where *1-Minute Habits* comes in. A 1-Minute Habit is a simple, positive action you do every day, for a minute or less. It is an action that coincides with your goal(s). It is purposefully designed to be ridiculously easy for you to do, so that the path to your goals will be aligned with the path of least resistance. This book will show you, with scientific evidence no less, that 1-Minute Habits well and truly are the best way to achieving lasting change.

1

You will learn that they indeed optimise our brains and get the most out of them.

The way our brains are actually designed makes them incompatible with our typical strategies. Yes, we fail and give up with our goals not because of some personal weakness of our own, but because we don't take into account how our brains actually work. So stop feeling guilty and hating yourself because it isn't your fault! You *can* achieve lasting change. All you have to do is work *with* your brain, instead of constantly *conflicting* with it. And this book will show you exactly how.

Many habit and self-help books I've read give great information and advice, but don't exactly show you HOW to change. They don't give any concrete practical advice for you to apply. I've read a lot of self-help and habit books and always found myself thinking after, "So now what?". I want to change that with this book. All the science and research is in here to convince you of its credibility. But I have also added very simple and practical steps for you to apply the *1-Minute Habits System*. Not only that but I have gone through lots of examples of popular habits and applied the system to them.

Whoever you are, and whatever your circumstances may be, I am certain you will find value in this book.

Out with the old, in with the new

Have you ever tried to accomplish a goal or set a New Year's Resolution but given up after a short while? Have you ever tried to do something over and over again (like lose weight or learn a new skill) but can never seem to maintain consistency? Have you ever felt like you don't have enough willpower, and aren't strong enough to accomplish what you want?

I know I have. It sucks when we try to pursue a goal and can't get there. You can't help but feel disappointed with yourself. And the more you try and fail, the worse you feel about yourself so you eventually stop trying completely.

But here's the thing, you don't have to feel like this anymore. The truth will indeed set you free. And the truth is that you aren't flawed, but your strategy is. For some of us, this will be hard to believe at first. It sure was for me.

We have been accustomed for so long to the ideas of setting big goals and 'diving into the deep-end'. We live in a society that promotes an 'All or Nothing' mentality when it comes to achieving big goals. But guess what? This 'All or Nothing' mentality conflicts with how our brains are actually designed!

Our culture promotes a goal strategy that goes against what scientific research advocates. It's no surprise why we are so quick to point fingers at ourselves for failing but not at our strategies. Societal norms and our pride end up clouding our judgement on how effective our strategies really are so we rarely ever think about changing them. We assume it's an innate problem of our own if they don't work. We think we can go all in, and then we end up so surprised and upset with ourselves when this doesn't work.

So what can we do that legitimately works? How about

adopting a strategy that coincides with scientific research? A strategy that revolves around neuroscience and psychology. A strategy that maximises the chance of consistency, and minimises the chance of failure. A strategy that optimises your brain.

We need this book because we need to understand that going after our goals doesn't have to be so damn hard. Most people (my past-self included), resign themselves to the idea that they aren't good enough and their goals are just fantasy. This book will show you that doesn't have to be the case. All you have to do is discard the old ways and bring in the new way.

By optimising your brain to be consistent with the right actions, you will get to where you want to be. You will reach fulfilment. The 7 chapters of this book will show you how.

Structure of *1-Minute Habits* and How to use it.

The book is divided into 2 distinct parts. Part 1 will show you the WHY. In the first 4 chapters you will learn everything you need to know about why you must use the 1-Minute Habits System over the regular method of setting Big Goals and relying on motivation.

Part 2 will show you the HOW. This part is fairly different from the first. It can be read like a reference guide where you can skim, or even skip over parts that you don't find applicable. However, I do recommend you read it all, just to get a broader understanding of how to apply the system.

Here's a closer look at what we will gain from each chapter.

Part 1: WHY

Chapter 1: Introduction to 1-Minute Habits
We will go through my story of how 1-Minute Habits came

4

to be, and why I needed them. We will also learn why our usual strategies tend to fail, and what a 1-Minute Habit is.

Chapter 2: The Brain
&
Chapter 3: Willpower, the Metaphorical Muscle

In these chapters we will explore the brain, habits, and willpower to help us get a deeper understanding of ourselves. This deeper understanding is imperative to learning how to optimise the brain.

Chapter 4: 1-Minute Habits Optimise the Brain

Everything will come together in this chapter. We will be fully convinced that our usual strategies really do constrain our brain. We will see why 1-Minute Habits are truly the best strategy to adopt to achieve lasting change.

Part 2: HOW

Chapter 5: Applying 1-Minute Habits

The foundation has been set by the previous 4 chapters. We'll know *why* we should form 1-Minute Habits. This chapter will show us *how*. It will take us through the 4 simple, yet deep, steps of the system so we can apply them.

Chapter 6: The Willpower Gym

Here, you will learn the most efficient and effective ways to strengthen your willpower, and what the most beneficial habits to form are.

Chapter 7: 1-Minute Habit Examples

The final chapter will show you conventional examples of how someone can apply the 4 steps of the system.

Final Words

After finishing the book, you will have all the info you need to start changing your life. This short section will end it with helpful reminders, and show you how you can join the 1-Minute Habits community.

Now, let's see how it all started.

Part 1: WHY

Chapter 1: Introduction to 1-Minute Habits

Faith is taking the first step even when you don't see the whole
staircase.
- Martin Luther King, Jr.

You cannot change your destination overnight, but you can
change your direction overnight.
- Jim Rohn

1.1. My Road to 1-Minute Habits

Experience: that most brutal of teachers. But you learn, my
God do you learn.
- C. S. Lewis

It was January 2014, and I had just gone through what can be
aptly surmised as a quarter-life crisis. For as long as I can
remember, negativity had slowly been building up within me
and I had pretty much reached my breaking point.

Most of my life, I've tried to bring about positive changes,
but to no avail. I've tried to exercise; I've tried learning new skills;
I've tried to close the gap between who I am, and who I want to
be. And yet each time I tried, I might've been able to progress for a
few weeks, maybe even months if I was lucky, but then I'd give up.
The burden, the tedium, and fear, all were just too much for me to
handle. I was overwhelmed.

Then I'd feel terrible and think I was too weak and
pathetic, which certainly didn't help. Time would go by and then
I'd suddenly get a burst of motivation and try again after a few
months. The same thing happened - I eventually got overwhelmed
and gave up, and then felt worse and worse.

In between these moments of working towards positive
changes and goals, I would find comfort with things that might be

considered 'bad habits'. I'd binge-eat, I'd excessively play video games, I'd stay up late on the computer, and I'd procrastinate constantly. Comfort was my safe-haven. I was obsessed with comfort. It was there for me when I couldn't do the things I wanted to. The more I escaped to my comfort, then the harder it became to get out of my comfort zone.

As years went by, these bad habits were accompanied by increasing stress and anxiety from not being able to accomplish the things I wanted to. I had big dreams, but little power to do them it seemed. But still, life wasn't all bad. I could handle these problems, and comfort was always there for me.

From Bad to Worse

Then it got worse. My bad habits and my anxiety were eventually joined by some health problems, a sleep disorder, and a digestive disorder. My digestive disorder made me very weak, but it was manageable. My sleep disorder though, made life extremely horrible.

And so years went by without being able to sleep properly. I foolishly waited a long time to go see a doctor about it too. But when I did, they couldn't really help, or diagnose it specifically so I never figured out what the problem was exactly. However, sleep maintenance insomnia and delayed sleep phase disorder (DSPD) fit the symptoms better than anything else. These disorders basically meant that I had trouble with falling asleep and staying asleep, and that my internal clock was distorted.

So I would be constantly sleep deprived. This sleep deprivation negatively affected my mood, work, relationships, health, and whole life. It made me cranky, tired, weak, stressed, irritable, and was turning me into the exact opposite of who I wanted to be. And the other issues in my life, like my digestive disorder, only exacerbated these negativities.

I really wanted to fix my sleep problem but, as in the past, working towards a self-created goal was something that I just couldn't seem to do. And unsurprisingly, my lack of sleep would make me too tired to even bother to try to fix the problem.

The awful state I was in would grow worse and worse over time. I was in a downward spiral and I didn't know how to get out. Then it got to the point where I couldn't take it anymore. January 2014 came, and my health, mood, and life had reached their lowest point. All the stress, anxiety, depression, and anger had built up and broke me down.

Time to change

Something had to change, and what better time to turn over a new leaf than a new year, right? However, I've tried countless times to bring lasting change with big goals and New Year's Resolutions and they never worked. Whether it was exercising; learning a new language; learning how to code; or fixing my sleep, I could never maintain consistency with them and would eventually give up.

But I knew that, this time, things would be different. Why? Because I had hit rock bottom. Hitting rock bottom (not like The Rock) provided me with a sense of urgency that I had never felt before. I wanted to find answers. I needed to find answers. How could I get a good night's sleep? Why couldn't I change for the better? What's the secret to achieving lasting change? My first priority was to fix my sleep of course.

Now the thing is, I still don't know how I got a sleep disorder and digestive disorder. Were they due to genetics or were they due to my lifestyle? It was hard to say. We can't control our genetics, but we can control our lifestyle. So with that in mind I realised it didn't matter if they were due to genetics. I knew that my lifestyle amplified the negative feelings, so I had to change something there.

A common piece of advice I'd get from friends and family was to just make myself tired through exercise and then I'd fall right to sleep. But it didn't matter how tired or exhausted my body felt as my mind would still keep me awake. And besides, as past experiences told me, I could never keep an exercise habit going on a consistent basis anyway.

Instead, I researched the causes of these disorders, and found that they both shared 'psychological factors', in other words, things like stress and anxiety. That doesn't mean these disorders are 'all in the mind'. There are various other potential causes, but psychological factors were shared by them both. So I wanted to kill 2 birds with 1 stone and decided to target my mind.

Anxiety was prevalent in my life, so what could I do to reduce it? Well in my research I came across exercise again, but I passed on that since it brought back the bad memories of constantly failing with it. Then I came across meditation.

Meditation

I was pretty intrigued by it. I've never tried it before but it didn't seem too difficult. After all, it's just sitting still, with eyes closed, and doing deep breathing. So that catered to my tired mind. Websites recommended doing around 10-15 minutes of meditation daily, and I was pretty motivated to change and was excited at all the benefits I'd get. So I tried. I tried and I failed miserably. I couldn't even make it past 2 minutes, and this was when I was highly motivated. Dammit. I tried again the next day; got nowhere near 10 minutes. Meditating is a lot harder than I thought. I just had no self-discipline, and was too fidgety and distracted. Then I wanted to try again the next day but couldn't be bothered at all. It just seemed like way too much effort. Too much effort that I wasn't even sure would work (or so I told myself). I came up with a load of excuses.

I couldn't be consistent and persevere with anything when my health was good, so it wasn't surprising that I couldn't do it now when my health was bad.

I was so used to the idea that strong people go all in and accomplish their tasks, no matter how hard or tedious it seems, so when I couldn't do this, I again felt pathetic. My pride made me feel like I could and should be able to do anything, and yet, once again, like all the other times in the past, my pride was wrong. I was upset, afraid, tired, and disappointed. And I gave up once again.

I lasted a few days with trying to meditate and then stopped trying completely. Talk about inconsistent. Why couldn't I persist and be consistent? It seemed like 2014 would follow the same cycle as previous years. But I was seriously sick and tired of it (literally and figuratively). I was sick of relying on feeling good to do things. And as I said above, I just knew that, this time, things would be different.

1-Minute Meditation

I then decided, out of some form of desperation, to do what I thought would be some pseudo reverse-psychology. My mind seemed to never want to work. But maybe I could trick it into starting and working or something like that. All I wanted, though, was not to be inconsistent anymore. I just wanted to start and feel like I was making some progress. Any progress. I told myself I'd only meditate for a minute. How could I pass this up? In a way, it felt like it was more effort *not* to do it.

So I set a timer, sat myself down, closed my eyes and focused on breathing. *BEEPBEEP*. Timer goes off; I open my

14

eyes and laugh at myself. Then I felt that, since I was already in the position to meditate, I might as well do a little bit more. I set a timer for 5 minutes this time. I didn't reach the 5 minutes, but when I stopped meditating I got up and felt strangely satisfied with myself. Next day rolls around and I decide to do the same thing. 1-Minute Meditation, let's go! There wasn't any resistance for me to start and so I did it with ease. And whilst I was in motion I would meditate for a little bit more again. I didn't know it at the time, but this would be the start of me learning about some literally life-changing information.

A few days went by and I managed to remain *consistent*. A few days turned into a week. I would always tell myself and expect myself to do just 1-Minute of meditation, but once I was in motion, I'd find it easy and do a little bit *extra*.

Glimmer of Hope

Around a month later, I was able to fall asleep a little bit quicker than I'm used to instead of rolling around in bed for hours!

I was pretty shocked. Although my sleep was far from perfect, I did feel a little better. Somehow I managed to be consistent *and* make progress in such a seemingly effortless manner. Why did this work over all the other strategies I'd tried in the past? Did my brain really fall for what I thought was 'reverse-psychology'? I had to know more.

I had never been so eager to learn before. The research led me to learn about how the brain actually works. I read studies, articles, and books about the brain's design and I came to some pretty shocking results.

What it showed me was that our typical ways of achieving goals just don't coincide with how our brains are designed. They actually conflict with it (more on this in chapter 4).

I had to see for myself if this was really true, and I didn't just get lucky with meditation. I decided to apply '1-Minute Habits' to other areas.

I did it

I decided to face an old nemesis: exercise. I was determined to see if my newfound strategy would work with it. And it did!

By getting myself to only do 1-Minute of Exercise, I was able to remain consistent and progress with it. By only planning to do 1-Minute, I was easily able to do *more* than a minute when I was in motion. Starting with 1-Minute I was finally able to see results with it - all without giving up. I was pretty shocked at how much progress I could make with something so seemingly easy.

With meditation and exercise both alleviating anxiety, my mind became calmer and more focused. I became healthier. Then guess what? 2 months after I started that 1-Minute Meditation, I was able to get a good night's sleep! Years of suffering with sleep deprivation, and all it bloody took was this simple strategy to make a difference. I was ecstatic. Again, my sleep wasn't completely perfect as the day after my sleep wasn't as good, but still, it gave me such strong hope that I CAN actually change, and that I CAN sort my life out. All those years of feeling hopeless and depressed led to this moment. I wasn't as weak as I had convinced myself I was.

As more time went by I would be further interested in the subject of the brain, habits, and willpower. The more research and books I read on them, the more I was able to refine the 1-Minute Habits System so that it can be applied by anyone, whatever their circumstances.

My sleep is now much better than it used to be, as well as my health, drive, and productivity. I'm a lot calmer and more focused. My body's in the best shape it's ever been. I am out of my downward spiral, and I know for sure, as more time goes by (as it's only been a few months), I will only get better and better.

With this system, I have also progressed with my other goals. I have formed fulfilling habits that will last me a long time. Along with the meditation and exercise habits, I have formed a 1-Minute Reading Habit where I've gone from reading around 1 book a year (awful I know) to 2-3 books a month. I've also formed a 1-Minute Writing Habit which led to this book. Yes, *1-Minute Habits* came from 1-Minute Habits. This book validates itself.

Now, that's enough of my story. This system has made me improve myself more than I ever have and I am confident it will help you do the same.

Next, we will look at why we keep repeating the same mistakes and what we should do about it.

1.2. Our usual strategies don't work

Whenever you find yourself on the side of the majority, it is time to pause and reflect.
- Mark Twain

If you do what you've always done, you'll get what you've always gotten.
-Tony Robbins

New Year's Resolutions

So, why aren't our usual strategies viable? Let's look at a common form of goal-achieving people try - New Year's Resolutions. New years are always exciting. We see them as a new chapter to our story. And the excitement and hype of a new year gets us pumped and feeling motivated. We feel ready to take on new challenges and improve ourselves. But as I, and many of us, have learnt from experience, New Year's Resolutions don't always work. Eventually the excitement wears off, our level of consistency drops, we feel overwhelmed, and then give up. When I first started looking into why 1-Minute Habits work and why my usual ways don't, I found 2 studies which showed that 88-92% of people fail in fulfilling their New Year's Resolutions.[1] Ouch. That's a *huge* proportion. So something is clearly wrong with the way we go about bettering ourselves. And yet we keep repeating the same mistakes over and over again.

Societal Norms

We are so accustomed to our strategies that we don't see anything wrong with them. We assume this because society endorses them. We are told that we can do anything, that we have no limits, that we can achieve anything if we want it bad enough etc. etc. All highly motivational and feel-good sayings. And they are all true to some extent. But the problem is that we misinterpret these ideals and revolve our strategies around them. Then we end up going all in, burning out, and giving up. This naturally leaves us feeling very surprised and disappointed in ourselves. Then we start feeling inadequate and believing we're not good enough. We kick ourselves and wish we had more willpower. We never think that the strategy is wrong because of how embedded it is in our heads. It makes sense that if one way doesn't work properly then we should try a different approach, right? And yet we don't do that with achieving goals.

We may alter the steps we take slightly but the overall strategy still focuses on big, overwhelming goals. Our insecurities make us constantly blame ourselves, and our dependence on societal norms keeps us from blaming them. These two then go hand in hand in preventing us from seeing what the true causes of our failures are. So what we need to do is stop looking in the wrong direction and start looking in the right one.

Consistency is Key

Let's stop focusing on achieving big goals inconsistently, and start focusing on achieving small progress consistently. Remember this: It is the accumulation of small progress that leads to big changes. It is not from constantly diving into the deep end; it is not from constantly going all in. Don't focus on a big future goal, focus on small present progress. Any progress, no matter how small, is infinitely greater than no progress at all.

I don't want to sound like I'm completely against big goals and dreaming big. No not at all. These things are great and essential for *direction* and for us to *visualise* where we want to be. These things are what can motivate us to start in the first place. Have Big Goals. Have Big Dreams. They are a catalyst that leads to great accomplishment. But once you've decided where you want to be, stop focusing on them, and start focusing on doing the things that'll get you there.

With our pride making us think we can do anything, and with our culture telling us to go all in, what happens is we are distracted by what really brings success: *Consistency*. We want to reach our goals real quickly. Too quickly in fact. Our impatience and pride makes us think that by doing more we can get there quicker. And this is also true. But we then try to change ourselves too much too quickly and end up failing, then either restarting at some later point in the future once we are motivated again, or we give up completely.

19

This typical approach is mired in inconsistency, the exact opposite of what achieving our goals requires! Instead of relying on our big goals to motivate us, and instead of waiting for when we feel good, we must focus on the process. We must focus on what actions we can do consistently to get us to our goal. We must focus on *Habits*.

Habits

Habits are the actions that we do consistently, triggered by a cue (signal or stimuli). It is a pattern that we regularly follow, until it feels almost involuntary. If you asked me, I'd tell you that our most defining traits are our habits. There is no greater indicator in determining who we are and where we may end up than our habits. Our thoughts and beliefs pale in comparison in defining us like our habits do. In fact, I'm going to go so far as to say that our thoughts and beliefs can essentially be worthless *if* they are not acted upon. They can be important in spurring us to act. However, we can think and believe in whatever we want, but that doesn't mean anything if we don't act in accordance with them.

It is our actions that show us and others what we truly think and believe. And it's our actions that have any redeemable value. And so the actions that we do repeatedly - our habits - show us and the world what we truly believe. Therefore, learning about and working on habits can be one of the most life-changing and important decisions we ever make.

I could even argue that some of the most successful, inspiring and creative people of the world got there due to their habits. Granted, we can also argue that luck, talent, circumstance, genetics, or up-bringing played a hand, but if you look deeper, the common denominator amongst *all* these people is that they had relevant habits and routines that coincided with their goals. It is the things they did consistently that played a huge part in getting them to where they are today. We can't fully control our luck, talents, circumstances, genetics, or up-bringing, unfortunately. But we can control our habits, which, again, is why they are so important.

But a lot of us have tried and failed with forming the right habits. The biggest trouble we have is with being consistent. And this is the main ingredient that we require. So what can we do about this?

Form 1-Minute Habits.

1.3. What are 1-Minute Habits?

A 1-Minute Habit is a scaled-down version of a habit you want to form, where your habit coincides with your goal(s). It is a small, easy, action you do every day that can be for a minute or less. It aligns your goal to the path of least resistance to maximise consistency. It is your habit enabler and gets you to start. They are so effortless that anyone can apply them, regardless of their circumstance. An important note: '1-Minute' Habits don't have to be confined to *time*. You can also use *quantity*. So '1-Minute of Writing' can be 'Write 1 paragraph', or 'Write 20 words'. Either way, it is something simple that can be done in a minute or less.

The whole 1-Minute Habits System is designed around simplicity, but you will see later that it is actually very intricately and cleverly designed. The system revolves around a plethora of significant scientific research to optimise our brains.

1-Minute Habits spur you to get out of your comfort zone, and get into motion. This in itself is great. You will be teaching yourself that what is outside your comfort zone really isn't all that uncomfortable, which will set a precedent for your current and future goals. 1-Minute Habits ease you into discomfort so won't

21

ever make you feel overwhelmed or burnt out. And once you are out of your comfort zone and in motion, you exponentially increase your chances of '*over-performing*'. This is because you will have built momentum. As you saw from my personal story, I would set out to do 1-Minute of a task, and then it would lead me into doing more than intended.

You only ever plan to do your 1-Minute Habit, and when you do, you will reach your quota for the day. You can stop there or you can over-perform (only if you want to). But you only decide to over-perform whilst in motion. You only decide to do more *during* or *straight after* your 1-Minute Habit, never before or a while after. You will understand why this is important in later chapters.

This over-performance is where you can do as much or as little as you want. You see, 1-Minute Habits will never restrain you from progressing. You might have thought that with 1-Minute Habits, progress will be very small or non-existent. That is not true at all. 1-Minute Habits **GUARANTEE** progress unlike other strategies. But how big and how small that progress is will be up to you, so it adds flexibility to make sure you remain consistent. Either way, you will be making some progress that can be built upon.

Over time, you will get better and better at over-performing since you will be constantly putting yourself in motion to do so. But if you don't want to over-perform on any day then you don't have to. Again this system's flexibility wants to maximise your consistency. And even if you never over-perform, you will still be forming a 1-Minute Habit. A little progress is infinitely greater than no progress. So if you never over-perform, and form solely a 1-Minute Habit you will have still built a foundation to work with and improve.

1.4. Big Goals vs. 1-Minute Habits

Our usual Big Goals strategy is good for giving us direction and helping us to visualise where we want to be. But what exactly is a Big Goal? If you look at them closely, you will see that they are simply a sum of small actions.

The problem is that we are too focused on the total sum and not on what makes up the sum. Realise this: The focusing on Big Goals strategy is only good for *planning* progress, whilst the 1-Minute Habits System is about *making* progress. 1-Minute Habits break the total sum of your goals down into small, actionable parts. Thereby allowing you to focus on what is important - consistency and repetition.

Let me contrast these 2 strategies a little more, by showing you more reasons why our old ways don't work, and why 1-Minute Habits do work.

4 reasons why we shouldn't focus on Big Goals

1) Big Goals put you in a state of continuous failure

You will set yourself a large goal, say losing a few jean sizes before summer or writing a book. And until you reach that goal (if you even reach it) you will be constantly reminded that you are short of your goal and, hence, not good enough.

These constant reminders of feeling inadequate and not good enough will place an unnecessary burden upon you and increase your levels of stress and anxiety which saps your energy. This is also known as ego-depletion which we will look at later on. All of this stress and anxiety sapping your energy makes it even harder for you to work on your goals, perpetuating further stress and anxiety which could put you in a negative feedback loop that ultimately results in giving up.

2) The success of reaching your Big Goals can be short-lived

In the beginning, your goal will give you direction and purpose. But what happens once you reach it? Of course you will celebrate and feel good about yourself, but then what? You will have lost the one thing that was driving you and motivating you. Now who's to say that the achievements of your goal will even last? If you haven't formed a habit out of it, it is very unlikely that you'll be able to maintain or go further with the progress you made. This means that it will be difficult to make any worthwhile long-term progress - progress that lasts. Then the only thing left is to set another goal to motivate you and restart the cycle of feeling like a 'continuous failure'.

3) Big Goals are difficult to plan for due to long-term unpredictability

We tend to underestimate the time it takes to complete a task or achieve a goal - known as the planning fallacy.[2] We also live in a state of flux. The world is ever-changing and unpredictable. And our own emotions and circumstances can be unpredictable, so it makes it increasingly difficult to control and plan for unforeseen things. This difficulty in controlling and planning makes this strategy inflexible.

4) Big Goals are focused in the future and so are disconnected to us

Big Goals are an abstract future hope. By focusing on them, and thereby focusing on the future, we are putting our brains in suspense which makes us anxious. And because they are so far away and distant from us, we feel disconnected to them. Without a connection to our goals, and without a focus on the present, we have to constantly try to motivate ourselves and constantly try to maintain our beliefs that we should go after them. This places an unnecessary burden upon us. We shouldn't rely on motivation anyway since it is unreliable. But without a connection to our goals, we need it. And when we don't feel motivated, the disconnection becomes ever more apparent, so much so that our drive to work on them gradually diminishes until we give up.

4 reasons why we should focus on 1-Minute Habits

1) 1-Minute Habits put you in a state of continuous success

1-Minute Habits utilise the scientifically-backed power of *Small Wins* (more on this in chapter 4). Once you reach your 1-Minute quota, you will have done your requirement for working on this habit and hence will achieve a small win. Not only that, but you are also likely to over-perform. So you will accumulate even more wins! What you get is a gradual building loop of constant wins. Your brain will become familiarised with wins and the positive feelings they bring and therefore will want to maintain consistency. What happens is you will end up in a positive feedback loop, the exact opposite of focusing on Big Goals. So you'll be in a state of continuous success that perpetuates further benefits and success.

2) 1-Minute Habits bring long-lasting benefits

Your goal will give you direction and vision. But by forming habits that coincide with this goal you will gain lasting change and lasting benefits. You won't need to worry about losing progress as the habit will be deeply ingrained into your brain (more on this in the next chapter). And since you have formed a habit, you can build upon it and go even further with your progress. This is because habits are energy efficient. Your brain will be so used to doing the habit that it doesn't require much thought in doing it and it will feel automatic. This means it will have energy saved that can be used on enhancing that habit and progressing further beyond. So habits will allow you to make long-term progress and then some.

3) 1-Minute Habits are easy to integrate and plan for

This goes without saying really as it's in the name. You'll stick with your daily quota of 1-Minute Habits because it is not taxing on your time and energy. No matter the state you'll be in, or your circumstances, you will feel very little resistance to remaining consistent and increasing your streak (number of days in a row you have done your 1-Minute Habit - more on this in chapter 5). And if you have the will to do so, you can over-perform.

The unpredictability of life is unlikely to hamper the integration of something as simple as the 1-Minute Habits System. And 1-Minute Habits also don't rely on our emotions (which can't always be trusted) either, so they can be done regardless of how we feel.

4) 1-Minute Habits are focused on the present and so we can connect to them

Instead of focusing on some future abstract goal, 1-Minute Habits focus on present action. Instead of 'losing weight' or 'reducing stress', you will instead do something like a '1-Minute Walk/Jog everyday', or a '1-Minute Meditation', respectively. 1-Minute Habits give you a defined, easy action to do, that when done repeatedly enough over time, will lead to your goal. And if you want to achieve your goal faster, you can over-perform, which is also focused only in the present. And more importantly, over-performance is focused only in the present whilst *doing* your 1-Minute Habit (more on this in chapter 5). So over-performance is literally focused right in the moment of when you are in already motion.

1 Minute Habits

By being focused solely on the present, we can connect and link ourselves with our 1-Minute Habits. We won't need to rely on motivation to do them because of this. And because they are so effortless to begin with they require minimal motivation as it is. This greatly increases the chances of us remaining consistent.

***

1-Minute Habits are all about getting you to start, getting you moving, and getting you to maintain consistency. It is by doing these things that get us closer to our goals. The point of this chapter was to contrast our old ways with the 1-Minute Habits System (more of this in chapter 4). It was to bring to light how it is our strategies, and not us, that go wrong. Our typical approach has been wrong for all these years. Entrepreneur James Clear says, "The typical approach is to dive into the deep end as soon as you get a dose of motivation, only to fail quickly and wish you had more willpower as your new habit drowns. The new approach is to wade into the shallow water, slowly going deeper until you reach the point where you can swim whether you're motivated or not."

If you are still feeling sceptical at this stage then that's normal, don't worry. I don't expect to fully convince you from my word alone. And I wouldn't want you to form 1-Minute Habits on blind faith. That's why in the next 2 chapters I will be going through the science of habits and willpower and going deep into our heads. We will be looking at the brain's relationship to habits, the parts of the brain responsible for habits, and our willpower and self-control. This will all culminate in us getting a better understanding of why we fail and what we should do about it.

1.5. Chapter 1 Key Facts

- We repeat the same mistakes over and over again whilst expecting different results – the definition of insanity.
- Societal norms and our insecurities are the reason we keep making the same mistakes. We blame ourselves, not our strategies.
- Consistency is the key to success.
- To achieve our goals we must focus on the journey, not the destination. Goals are the destination. Habits are the journey.
- 1-Minute Habits are your journey, simplified.
- There are a lot of flaws in focusing on big goals. 1-Minute Habits counter these flaws.

Chapter 2: The Brain

When we look at living creatures from an outward point of view, one of the first things that strike us is that they are bundles of habits.
- William James

We are what we repeatedly do. Excellence, then, is not an act, but a habit.
- Will Durant

2.1. Understanding the Brain and Habits

If we want to really learn about how habits work and how best to form them, then we're going to have to learn about the brain. The brain as a subject can seem pretty daunting since it's so complex. The brain is filled with meticulous intricacies that neuroscientists have yet to figure out. Due to its complexities, it can seem intimidating and confusing for people to talk and learn about it. It's no wonder that significant insights and breakthroughs about the brain aren't shared by the general media. However, the good news is that we don't need to understand all the intricacies of the brain to understand how habits work.

What's more is that there has been a tremendous influx of research on the brain over the past few decades, shedding light on some of its mysteries. We are at a pivotal point in time where we can better understand how to improve ourselves. The problem, though, is that a lot of the research is scattered and filled with scientific jargon (understandably) so it is difficult to apply. Not only that, but most of us don't have the time and energy to go through the vast amount of research there is to find out what may be useful. These insightful findings would be of more use if they were transcribed colloquially so we could have a simple breakdown of them. This would get us to understand why we go wrong, and get us to follow a path that scientifically works.

I will aim to provide this *simplified* breakdown of the information that you need to know. It would be too much for the scope of this book to go into all the details of the brain and it would also be extremely unnecessary. I will transcribe the information that is vital to understanding the brain, habits, willpower, and how 1-Minute Habits fit into all of this. Throughout the book, I cite articles and peer-reviewed studies of significance and *briefly* go through them to give you a good understanding of what their key findings were. Of course, if you would like to learn more about the studies, then simply follow the sources I provide in the References section. Note though, that most studies contain a *lot* of jargon.

Now let's look at the brain.

The Brain

The reason why our usual strategies don't work is because they are not designed with our physiology in mind. We try to change too much too quickly (go all in, dive into the deep end). What we don't realise is this goes against our primal instincts. With our usual strategies, we go up against thousands upon thousands of years of human evolution. We got to this point in time through small, gradual changes over the course of millions of years! So our brains are really not hard-wired to change in an instant, and yet we keep trying to do just that.

I've talked about the brain a lot without explaining it. So what is the brain?

The brain is the front and centre controller of our nervous system - a network which coordinates all our actions and transfers signals all over the body. It contains billions of neurons which process and transmit information via electrical and chemical signals. How this information is transmitted is via synapses which are the 'pathways' of our nervous system. An internal or external cue (internal or external signal) can set off certain synapses to trigger certain actions. Sounds a bit confusing, but don't worry.

The Brain and Habits

When a cue triggers an action, what goes on in our brain? The cue triggers an electrical charge in the brain which travels along a pathway associated with a specific action. When we *constantly repeat* an action, the pathways associated with that action become bigger and stronger. So habits have strong pathways. These stronger pathways make the *transfer of information* easier, and therefore require less energy. Our brain will constantly try to conserve energy to the best of its ability (due to the primal instinct of survival) so it will 'automatically' fall back on those repeated actions, especially when it's tired. Hence why I mentioned earlier that our brain looks for the path of least resistance.

Now let me give you a quick example. Take the action of brushing your teeth. It's a habit we repeatedly do. In your brain, you will have a neural pathway associated to the specific act of brushing your teeth. So when you wake up, or before you go to bed, a cue triggers your brain to perform this action. From having constantly repeated this action, we find that brushing our teeth can feel 'automatic' or 'involuntary'. It doesn't take a lot of conscious effort to do. And the less conscious effort something takes the likelier our brain is to do it because it wants to conserve energy.

How long does it take to form a habit?

We want to form the right habits. What we need to do then is initiate the pathways of the relevant actions and strengthen them via repetition. Easier said than done. So how long do we have to repeat an action for until it becomes a habit? How long do habits take to form? Well the short answer is it depends on the habit and the level of consistency.

The most significant study to answer this question was from the *European Journal of Social Psychology*[3]. In this study the participants were tasked with performing an eating, drinking, or exercise behaviour of their choosing every day for 12 weeks (84 days). Examples of the behaviours chosen were 'eating a piece of fruit with lunch', 'drinking a bottle of water with lunch' and 'running for 15 minutes before dinner'. So their cues would be constant throughout the 84 days as well (with lunch, before dinner and so on).

What they found was that the *average* time it took was 66 days. Pretty good to know. But their range was between 18 to 254 days. Oh.

So there is no definitive answer. It varies a lot depending on the habit itself and the level of consistency. Some could take 20 days in a row, some could take 200. An important takeaway though is that forming a habit isn't like switching a light bulb on. It isn't a sudden change. It is gradual and subtle. So even if your action doesn't become fully automated, say after 35 days in a row, it doesn't mean that you haven't progressed or benefited. For example, it will be much easier to do your action on Day 35 than Day 1. And assuming all other variables remain the same, it will be easier to do your action on Day 35 than on day 34 too, but the difference may be too subtle to notice. Gradually the subtle progress builds up, and will form into a habit, so each day will be progress.

The study also revealed that missing a day did not derail the process of habit-formation. But obviously making a 'habit' out of missing days won't be good at all. The more consistent you are, the quicker your progress will be. The good thing is that 1-Minute Habits are so easy to do that the only way you'll miss a day is if you forget to do them as opposed to not being bothered to do them. Forgetting them will be unlikely too since they coincide with your goals and so will be important to you. In chapter 5 we will learn about a technique that will ensure we won't forget to do our 1-Minute Habits, and provide us with a whole range of other benefits.

Even though there is no definitive answer, when you perform repetition in an action, you will gradually see signs that it is becoming a habit. This means you can get an idea on how much progress has been made and how long it may take you to fully form the habit.

What are the signs of habit-formation?

Habits are defined as being almost involuntary and automatic. So we have to look for signs of *automaticity*. According to Social Psychologist John Bargh, there are 4 characteristics that usually accompany automaticity, although not all need to be present. These are: efficiency, awareness, controllability, and intentionality.[4]

So when we are repeating an action, we should look for: How much effort the mental process requires; how aware or unaware we are with the mental process taking place; whether we can stop or change the process midway into it; and how intentional the mental process is.

As actions are repeated in consistent settings (cues) they gradually become more *efficient* as they require less energy and thought. Since our brain becomes used to the action there is less need to oversee the process of it. So our subconscious takes over and we feel *unaware* of it. From repeating actions in consistent settings our *control* of the behaviour transfers to cues in the environment that activate an automatic response. By transferring control, the *intentionality* of the action falls. Habits increase efficiency of the action, and reduce the awareness, control, and intentionality of it.

Habits initially take self-control and energy to form. Once they are formed, though, that energy is freed up to be used elsewhere, either on improving your already formed habit, or in other areas. So habits are a way to conserve energy and progress very effectively and efficiently.

Good habits vs. Bad habits

It's great to have good habits. Our mind can automate us into positive behaviours without much effort on our part. But then there are bad habits. We all struggle with temptations, distractions and procrastination. When we are automated into doing these actions, it is because they are the path of least resistance. A primal instinct of our brain is to conserve energy and do what it thinks is best for survival. Yes, when you are tempted by cake, your brain 'thinks' that eating it and getting that sugar rush is better for its survival than, say, working out or eating healthily.

You might start questioning the design of our brains and wonder how they can seem so stupid. Well, the fact is that our brains simply haven't evolved quick enough to keep up with the rapidly changing world we live in today. They are more used to catering towards short-term day-to-day survival from starvation, disease, and predators rather than how many times we go to the gym, or how much time we spend on learning.

So must we break these bad habits? Well, it's a little more complicated than that. You may or may not have noticed, but I have been focusing on the idea of *forming* new habits instead of *breaking* old ones. Why? Because it is scientifically more viable to form new habits than to break old ones. Earlier, I described how habits work in relation to our brain. When we repeat an action often enough, the synaptic pathways of that action grow stronger and bigger. We can weaken these synaptic pathways if we stop repeating the corresponding action, but the reason breaking bad habits is more difficult than forming new ones is because these pathways never actually go away - the habit can be reactivated with only a slight provocation.[5]

Anyone who's tried to quit smoking can vouch for this. They can go months or even years without a cigarette, and then give in just one time and find that their bad habit is back in full force. Therefore, it's optimal to form a good habit to replace the bad habit. When you find certain cues that trigger your old bad habits, you'll have the good habit there to fall on.

Also, breaking bad habits tends to involve suppression. For example, dieters may work on breaking the bad habit of binge-eating chocolate by suppressing their urges instead of trying to find a positive habit to replace it with. Many studies show that suppression and prohibition don't actually work[6]; are bad for you[7]; and lead to a greater chance of relapse.[8] Resistance, therefore, can truly be futile.

So, although we can apply a form of the 1-Minute Habits System to breaking bad habits, I strongly recommend you stick with only *forming* habits instead of *breaking* them. *1-Minute Habits* will solely focus on the former as it is most viable for success and most optimal.

***

We've taken in a lot of information about habits.

We know that we should focus on forming habits, we know what signs to look out for, and we know that habits *may* take an average of 66 days. And how we form habits is through repetition.

Is repetition the magic pill then? Well, yes and no. It sounds obvious and simple to say that for us to form the right habits we have to be repetitive and consistent in our actions. This is true. However, as we all probably have experienced first-hand, it isn't as easy as it sounds. Typical strategies like focusing on big goals and going all in don't take into account external circumstances and, more importantly, don't take into account our internal circumstances.

We have to go even deeper. We will look at the 2 most prominent players in our brains that are responsible for habit-formation: The automater, basal ganglia, and the habit-former, pre-frontal cortex.

2.2. Basal Ganglia

First of all, I would like you to picture the human brain as an onion - with lots and lots of layers. In the human brain, these layers are made up of neural cells. Now, the outermost layer of the brain, the parts closest to the scalp, is what we call the cerebral cortex, also known as grey matter and the 'thinking' part of the brain. This is where all your complex thoughts, ideas, beliefs, and opinions occur. Evolutionarily speaking, scientists see this outside layer of the brain as its most recent addition.[9] When we look deeper into the brain, we find structures that are a lot older and more primitive. The one we are interested in right now is located near the core of our onion brain. What we'll find here is an oval of cells called the basal ganglia.

When a cue triggers a negative habit, it is the basal ganglia and motor neurons at work resulting in the automaticity that we all find so difficult to control. It is the part of the brain that makes us do things without much conscious thought that we end up regretting, like binge-eating or procrastinating. It doesn't care about our goals and what we truly want, and it doesn't differentiate between what is beneficial for us and what is harmful. All it cares about is patterns. It detects and craves patterns (the things that we do repeatedly) to conserve our energy. So it can seem pretty frustrating when this 'pattern detector' seems to make our mind work against us as we fall into a bad habit automatically.

However, this basal ganglia is also the reason our good behaviours become automated. For instance, it doesn't seem draining to have to grab the toothpaste, squeeze it out onto your brush, and start brushing, does it? Or do we have to pause and think about how to breathe? How easy is it to drive a car after a few years of experience? When we first start driving, our brain has so much to take in and our concentration requires straining effort. But once you're used to it, the basal ganglia takes over and you are a lot more relaxed and able to divert your attention to other things. So we may not like it when it automates us into doing things we regret, but without it we would be in deep trouble.

The basal ganglia is a main player in what determines when to let habits and automation take over.[10] Without it, we would feel constantly overwhelmed by all the little decisions we would have to make such as walking or breathing, and our brains would shut down. Without it, we would constantly have to relearn everything as we wouldn't be able to form habits. Damaged basal ganglias are associated with Parkinson's and Huntington's disease, as well as other brain disorders.[11]

It is from consistency that our basal ganglia detects patterns, so inconsistent actions for big goals do not work with this part of the brain. The main problem, though, is that it doesn't know which consistent actions benefit us and which harm us. It is responsible for *unconscious automatic* decisions and *doesn't* care about our goals.

However, there is a part of our brain that *is* responsible for our *conscious* decisions and *does* care about our goals - the pre-frontal cortex. So if we want the basal ganglia to automate the habits that coincide with our goals, then we're going to have to also understand how the pre-frontal cortex works.

2.3. Pre-frontal Cortex

The pre-frontal cortex, located in the front part of your brain, behind your forehead, is proclaimed by many authors to have an integral link to our personality.[12] This part of our brain is what we'd associate with who we are.

Many studies have also led to the pre-frontal cortex being labelled as the self-control centre of the brain.[13] So it is where we derive our willpower (willpower and self-control are used interchangeably) from. Its main tasks are to carry out *executive functions*: it differentiates between good and bad thoughts and determines what is best for you; recognises future consequences of actions; works towards goals; and suppresses urges. It plays an integral role in our short-term thinking, planning, and decision-making. And it has the ability to override the basal ganglia so it can prevent us from becoming automated into doing negative things and make us do positive things instead.

Sounds amazing, right? So why do we constantly falter on the path of forming the right habits and changing for the better? Well, the reason for that is because its energy (what we refer to as willpower) is limited.[14]

As you can see from its description above, the pre-frontal cortex has a big burden on its shoulders from all its executive responsibilities, and therefore requires a lot of energy. Once this limited energy is depleted, in comes the basal ganglia to automate actions to conserve that remaining energy as much as possible.

To create the positive habits that we want, we need to take into account the characteristics of our pre-frontal cortex and basal ganglia. We have to make our pre-frontal cortex override the basal ganglia and repeatedly do positive actions until they become habit. Once they become habitual they won't require much energy and the basal ganglia will automate it, saving energy for our pre-frontal cortex to use for other positive functions. But for the pre-frontal cortex to repeatedly override the basal ganglia requires consistent energy, so how are we supposed to do that when its energy seems so limited?

We must first ask why it is limited, which is exactly what the next chapter looks into. We will look deeper into the valuable resource of willpower. This knowledge will help us to fully understand where we go wrong in trying to achieve lasting change.

2.4. Chapter 2 Key Facts

- The main priority of the brain is survival.
- Habits conserve energy and are conducive to survival, so the brain prefers habits over big goals.
- The Basal Ganglia is our habit automater, but it doesn't differentiate between good and bad habits.
- The Pre-frontal Cortex is our habit creator, but its energy (willpower) is limited.

Chapter 3: Willpower, the Metaphorical Muscle

Will is character in action.
- William McDougall

There is no such thing as a great talent without great will power.
- Honore de Balzac

3.1. Willpower and Ego-depletion

At its essence, willpower (a.k.a self-control) is the ability to delay gratification. With it, you can resist short-term temptations in order to meet long-term goals.

Roy Baumeister, a Professor of Psychology, is a highly renowned, highly influential, and highly cited researcher[15] for his numerous works on self-control, and self-regulation. It is his research that led to the development of the theory of *Ego-Depletion* and the strength-model of self-control which states that willpower is like a muscle.

In his book, *Willpower: Rediscovering our Greatest Strength*, he claims that willpower - the ability to control impulses and thoughts, and persevere with tasks - is a *limited* resource that gets depleted over the course of the day as more mental activity occurs.

He coined the term ego-depletion to describe this theory which is just a fancy term for willpower/self-control reduction throughout the day. To prove this theory, he conducted a number of experiments[16] which showed that ego-depletion has a spillover effect - using self-control in one area uses up a limited source of energy, and so may hinder a subsequent task that requires self-control. For example, if you resist the temptation to eat chocolate, you may find it more difficult later on to persist in a task.[17] Or if you enact self-control to make yourself more productive at work and ignore distractions, then you may find it more difficult to work out after work. Therefore, our willpower can help in immediate situations, but this comes at a cost - loss of control later on as the day progresses.

Many other studies and over 100 experiments support this result (and we'll look at a few more of these studies in the next section).

Using willpower in one area limits our ability to use it in others due to willpower itself being a *limited* resource. All decisions and self-control tasks drain energy from the same source - our willpower reserve.

Willpower is 'like' a Muscle

From these studies and more, the strength-model of self-control was born[18], which compared ego-depletion to the fatigue one gets from physically using a muscle. It gets tired the more you use it, just like a muscle. One task that strains our willpower muscle will tire it out, making it less effective for subsequent tasks. But like a muscle it can also be replenished with rest and food. So if we tire out our willpower muscle throughout the day, eating some healthy food, and getting a good night's sleep can bring our willpower back to normal levels. That is fortunate since if we couldn't replenish our willpower, then each act of ego-depletion would be permanent, and then we'd eventually stop functioning completely!

Where our typical strategies falter the most is in not taking into account the limitations of the brain. They don't take into account how the brain functions and how habits really work. They don't realise that willpower is actually limited, and not infinite like our culture perpetuates.

The next section will show you what exactly weakens willpower. It will show the exact main causes of ego-depletion and what exactly makes our willpower muscle get tired. Once we learn the answers, we will begin to see more clearly how 1-Minute Habits well and truly optimise our brains and are the best system to adopt to change ourselves for the better.

3.2. What exactly weakens willpower?

We have to make sure our willpower reserves are not depleted when it comes to forming habits. If we need willpower to form habits, then we must know how to optimise our limited willpower. So let's look at what depletes it.

Decision Fatigue

A prevalent cause of ego-depletion is decision fatigue. This fatigue is caused by one having too many choices and decisions to make. Just as ego-depletion hampers our ability to do a subsequent task, decision fatigue hampers our ability to make subsequent decisions - the more decisions we make, the worse our decisions gradually become.[19]

We've all most likely already experienced and intuitively understand ego-depletion and decision fatigue. It is what we all tend to experience after a long, tiring day of work. For some of us, work consists of sitting at a desk, using a computer for hours, yet we subjectively feel physically and mentally drained after a hard days' work. Coming home feeling tired or stressed leaves us depleted of willpower, and we show less restraint in our decisions. We go into auto-pilot mode and cave in to short-term impulses, such as becoming short-tempered with our family, and munching on cookies. When your willpower is depleted, parts of your brain become slower and muted. It's as if your pre-frontal cortex falls asleep, which leads to your basal ganglia stepping in. So, our quality of decision-making tends to drop, our pre-frontal cortices feel drained and tired, and we end up making poorer decisions that may hamper our long-term plans.

Ego-depletion and Blood Glucose

Decision fatigue, and ego-depletion in general, impairs our self-control and reduces our willpower reserve because it reduces our blood glucose.[20] Blood glucose refers to a sugar that supplies energy to all the cells in our bodies. If a reduction in blood glucose levels reduces our willpower, then can't we just increase our blood sugar levels to increase our willpower? Well the answer to that is yes.[21] But it is only a temporary and short-term fix. Depending on high blood sugar levels to constantly maintain willpower is unfortunately unstable, and increases the chances of problems like tooth decay and weight gain - and all the other problems associated with it like heart disease and diabetes.[22]

All decisions affect willpower

All decisions (conscious and subconscious) deplete our willpower. From choosing what to eat for breakfast, how to spend your work breaks, how to spend your money at the shops, to deciding parole for prisoners if you're a judge[23], and how much you resist your urges, it all depletes our willpower. As the day goes by and more decisions and choices are made, we become more impulsive and gradually favour short term gains and delayed costs. The media, and our favourite companies and shops take advantage of our decision fatigue as well. For instance, notice how chocolates and candies are placed near the cash registers in grocery stores. Grocery shopping involves a lot of decisions and choices to be made, which lower our glucose levels. This makes our brains crave a quick hit of sugar. Companies know we are tempted by the sweet, sugary snacks at this stage and capitalise on our impaired state.[24] Cheeky.

Decision Fatigue and the Information Age

What's scary about decision fatigue, though, is that it affects us in this day and age more than ever. Choices and decisions to be made are in sheer abundance. With the constant influx of information and our incessant need to stay updated, we peruse our favourite websites, social networks, news outlets, and so on, and receive overwhelming amounts of information that we take in, and with it, more and more choices and decisions to make. Deciding on what news story to read, or whose profile to stalk on Facebook, choosing which YouTube video to watch, or deciding whether you should check your phone and reply to someone's message - it all depletes our willpower.

The effect on our willpower from clicking on one extra profile on Facebook, or watching one extra video on YouTube isn't concrete and obvious. It is difficult for anyone to see how tiring a decision makes us, even if that decision is an intense one. But regardless of the intensity of a decision, it all adds up to greater willpower depletion. That's why in this day and age, we must be conscious and aware of all the distractions around us and all the information we take in as its negative effect can be subtle but have profound long-term effects if we're not careful: Too much information will make us experience decision fatigue, which can make us more impulsive and cater to negative, short-term whims. And if we are impulsive and short-sighted on a consistent level, we will form bad habits that can damage our lives. So moderation is key.

Meta-analysis on Ego-depletion

Unfortunately, decision fatigue is not the only thing that hampers our willpower reserve. An ego-depletion meta-analysis (which is research that examines other studies to identify patterns and relationships) of 83 studies found the 5 factors that have the most significant effect on ego-depletion.[25] These factors are effort; perceived difficulty; negative affect; subjective fatigue; and blood glucose levels.

So any decision or action we make that involves *effort* or is *perceived* to be difficult will reduce our willpower. Any thought or decision of our own or any externality that *negatively* affects us will reduce willpower. How *subjectively tired* we feel reduces our willpower. And lower levels of *blood glucose* deplete our willpower.

No matter what, our willpower will deplete throughout the day due to our actions and due to externalities. And some things deplete our willpower more than others. As long as we manage it and do our best to conserve our willpower then we're fine. But the problem is that in our lives we are very wasteful with our willpower. But it doesn't have to be that way.

In the next chapter we will look at all the reasons why 1-Minute Habits optimise the brain.

3.3. Chapter 3 Key Facts

- Willpower is like a muscle. It gets tired over the course of the day due to ego-depletion.
- It is not infinite.
- Ego-depletion comes in various forms: decision fatigue; effort; perceived difficulty; negative affect; subjective fatigue; and lower blood glucose.

Chapter 4: 1-Minute Habits Optimise the Brain

Great things are done by a series of small things brought together.
- Vincent Van Gogh

The will is the keystone in the arch of human achievement. It is the culmination of our complex mental faculties. It is the power that rules minds, men and nations.
- Thomas Parker Boyd

4.1. Small Wins

One of the major ways the 1-Minute Habits System optimises the brain is in its embodiment of Small Wins. What are small wins? Well, they're exactly what they sound like. By accomplishing any small feat or making incremental progress, you will achieve a small win.

I mentioned that our usual strategy involves us constantly feeling like a failure because we haven't reached our goal yet. *1-Minute Habits* flip that approach on its head and utilise the concept of small wins to get us feeling like constant winners instead of failures. Making progress on a task produces positive feelings of accomplishments and raises our self-esteem which fuels the fire of momentum.

Constantly feeling like the goal is so far away from our reach and feeling bad for not being there yet is detrimental to success as it increases our burden, pressure, and stress levels needlessly. Of course, some stress and pressure can be good for us, but most of the time we tend to overwhelm ourselves to the point of failure and never bother trying again.

Organisational theorist Karl Weick argued that perceiving challenges as large and inconvenient (big goals) made people feel paralysed, stressed, and overwhelmed. He indirectly found that simply perceiving or thinking about a difficult challenge can deplete our willpower.[26] Giving social examples from business, politics, gay rights, feminism, and environmentalism, he shows a variety of settings wherein small wins have been conducive to success. He states that "Once a small win has been accomplished, forces are set in motion that favour another small win." They initiate a snowball effect that turns into a positive feedback loop (which we'll look at in the next section). So if we want to change the world, then we shouldn't focus on changing the world; we should focus on small wins. The same principle applies to us. If we want to change ourselves, we must focus on small wins.

In the book *The Progress Principle*, Psychologists Teresa Amabile and Steven Kramer collected data on the moods and activities of people at work at 7 companies, and found that feeling like you are achieving incremental progress is vastly more important to success and happiness than either a large long-term goal or financial incentives. They also found that seemingly small signs of progress will induce huge positive effects on our psyches. But also, seemingly, small setbacks can induce huge negative effects as well.

What is also noteworthy from the book is that the feeling of success and happiness you get from accomplishing a task is *disproportionate* to the actual size of the task. In other words, achieving an important accomplishment that seems to be 100 times bigger in scope and challenge compared to a small win won't make you feel 100 times happier and fulfilled.

Charles Duhigg, in his acclaimed book *The Power of Habit*, also mentions something similar. He wrote that "Small wins have enormous power, an influence disproportionate to the accomplishments of the victories themselves." He then states, "Small wins fuel transformative changes by leveraging tiny advantages into patterns that convince people that bigger achievements are within reach." So it is more efficient and makes more sense to work on small wins consistently, and accumulate the positive benefits, as opposed to working on big wins inconsistently.

1-Minute Habits are the personification of small wins. It is more viable to focus on small wins than big goals. By reaching our daily quota of something as ridiculously easy as 1-Minute Habits, we will consistently amass small wins. And by over-performing we will gain even more wins. This idea of taking small steps is hardly a new one. But what a lot of us never realised is just how optimal it truly is to take change 1 step at a time. In the next section we will look at small wins a little bit more and how 1-Minute Habits put us into an optimal positive feedback loop.

4.2. Positive Feedback Loop of Small Wins

The 1-Minute Habits System is optimal due to taking into account our brain's limitations (which we'll look at after this section) and because it provides a positive feedback loop. In this section we will look at the latter. This feedback loop is possible due to 1-Minute Habits embodying small wins. From doing 1-Minute Habits consistently, we experience a cycle of benefits and improvements that grow bigger over time. Let's look at what the positive feedback loop involves.

Start

There's usually a lot of resistance involved when we want to start a seemingly uncomfortable task. 1-Minute Habits work around this issue. The point of the 1-Minute Habit is to be an initiator, a habit to start your habit. How can we expect ourselves to constantly work on a habit (or anything worthwhile really) if we haven't got the habit of starting ingrained in us?

Most of us tend to wait for ourselves to feel good or motivated to start. Most of us wait until we're 'ready'. Most of us wait until conditions are ideal. But let me tell you, this is completely counter-productive. People who think like that will have great difficulty in getting what they want out of life. This notion of waiting for, or relying on, ideal conditions is something I have had immense trouble with in the past and is something that I strongly feel impedes our progress.

Remember this: We'll never be truly 'ready'. Conditions will never be perfect. And if they are, those moments are so fleeting that relying on them will be completely inconsistent. Ideal conditions rely on ideal emotions. Our emotions, though, are erratic and fluctuate. We can't rely on them to start working. The best of us don't wait for ideal conditions. They just start. And 1-Minute Habits reshapes the brain to get it to continuously start with ease, reshapes it so that it doesn't need to ever wait for ideal conditions, or to feel good to carry out the positive actions that matter to you.

They minimise the resistance to start to maximise your ability to do so. And so you'll be in a positive loop of constantly starting, which means you'll gradually form the habit of starting which will help you start more and more.

Out of Your Comfort Zone

We know the brain doesn't like change. We know it wants to conserve as much energy as possible to survive. So it's going to put up a big fight and a lot of resistance to stop itself from doing 'uncomfortable' things. You see, your brain *LOVES* comfort. Comfort is the epitome of energy conservation and what your brain correlates with survival (since you wouldn't feel comfortable if you thought you were in danger). However, it is only by doing uncomfortable things that we can get the things we truly want. That's why we have to ease our brains into discomfort. We have to make the uncomfortable comfortable.

1 Minute Habits

We all have 3 types of comfort zones according to bestselling author MJ Ryan. In her book *This Year I Will...* she wrote that there are 3 zones of existence: comfort, stretch, and stress. Our comfort zones are where a lot of us reside. Our stress zones are way far out of our comfort zones and make us feel overwhelmed. They are what we dive into when we use the 'big goals' approach. The stretch zone, which is in between these zones, is where the magic happens. It is where discomfort can become comfort. She also states that consistently getting out of our comfort zones - getting into the stretch zone - keeps our brains healthy, sharp, and can prevent brain diseases like dementia.

To improve ourselves, we have to gently get out of our comfort zones and get into our stretch zones. Daniel H. Pink, the bestselling author of *Drive: The Surprising Truth About What Motivates Us* wrote that "We need a place of productive discomfort. If you're too comfortable, you're not productive. And if you're too uncomfortable, you're not productive. Like Goldilocks, we can't be too hot or too cold." Our comfort zones are too cold, and our stress zones (big goals) are too hot. What's optimal is to put ourselves in between. We have to find what is just right.

1-Minute Habits put us in the stretch zone. They make discomfort productive, and they make discomfort comfortable.

Like with starting, if you can consistently make yourself get out of your comfort zone, then just about anything will be easier for you to face. 1-Minute Habits minimise discomfort to maximise the chances for you to get out of your comfort zone. By scaling down your goals and doing your 1-Minute Habits, you will be *familiarising* yourself with the discomfort that your brain usually resists. You will begin to reshape its perceptions on these discomforts, fears, and resistances. 1-Minute Habits break down these barriers, so that what was met with seemingly insurmountable resistance will become the path of least resistance.

This makes it more likely for you to keep getting out of your comfort zone and keep increasing your confidence, which, in turn, makes it more likely that you will do your 1-Minute Habits and over-perform. Win-Win.

Motivation

Even though 1-Minute Habits help you to lose your reliance on waiting for ideal conditions or waiting for motivation, they themselves provide us with motivation. By minimising the resistance to starting due to their ease, they raise our perceived skill levels. From their ridiculous simplicity, they will positively affirm into our minds that "*I can do this easily*". Their minimised effort affirms "*That's all it takes*", and their minimised chance of failure affirms "*This is no big deal*".

By aligning motivation (and all the small wins) with the task at hand, the brain's reward system will start to correlate this 'discomfort' with positivity and feeling good, thereby increasing the chances of doing your task even more. Again it aligns and reshapes your brain into turning the uncomfortable into comfortable.

With 1-Minute Habits, you don't need motivation or courage to start. Instead you'll get them *after* you do them, instead of relying on them *before*.

It's Possible

By gaining these benefits, you will be consistently testing your comfort. You will be familiarising yourself with the resistance that you try to avoid, and will perceive that resistance in a new light. You will unravel it. You will gradually see that what you resist isn't actually as scary, uncomfortable, and difficult as you thought. And as you gradually break down that barrier, what will be left between you and your goal?

This leads to one of the most profound and important experiences we all need when trying to achieve anything. The experience that tells us *it's possible*. Our usual approach can make us feel impatient and leave us wondering whether it's going to be worth it. The disconnection with our goals and lack of consistent wins makes us lose hope, and doubts start to creep in. We then lose motivation because we don't think it's possible. When this happens, we eventually give up.

1-Minute Habits, on the other hand, will affirm into your mind that it's possible. You will become connected to your goal and start seeing that it isn't unreachable, that what you want is waiting, that it's possible. Your belief in yourself will become stronger and your belief in achieving your goal will become stronger. And with this strong belief you will be coinciding an *optimal* (which we'll look at next) action with it. Our beliefs empower our actions. And our actions empower our beliefs. 1-Minute Habits will empower both.

You will start experiencing a sense that it's possible with all the small wins you accumulate. These small wins will fuel more change, make you feel more accomplished, confident, and happier with yourself. They will make you feel more fulfilled.

This positive feedback loop will make it easier for you to remain *consistent* and do more. Because you'll want to be consistent and do more. Why? Because it's possible.

Forming a Habit that coincides with your Goal

All these benefits, and I haven't even mentioned the benefit that matters most to you - your actual habit and goal. 1-Minute Habits provide all these benefits AND they improve your ability to do your habit by promoting consistency. Like any habit, forming it makes it automatic and so you will have freed up energy and willpower to use on taking it further or on other things. 1-Minute

Habits gradually get you to your automaticity without burdening you unnecessarily.

**

All of these small wins make you progress, feel good, diminish resistance, and show you it's possible. This all in turn reinforces, complements, and enhances the positive feedback loop to make it increasingly accumulate all of the benefits. You will internalise the loop and be in an upward spiral. This is to optimise your ability to maintain consistency and over-perform. Remember: Consistency that coincides with your goals is key.

4.3. Big Goals and 1-Minute Habits vs. Ego-depletion

So we've seen the positivity of small wins and how they reinforce that it is the accumulation of small changes that leads to success. And we've seen that we should adopt 1-Minute Habits so that we can experience their positive feedback loop. Now I'm going to bring it all full circle, and show you why our brains fully thrive with 1-Minute Habits.

From looking deep into the brain and understanding it, we came to the key finding that our willpower is limited and experiences ego-depletion from any subsequent task. For a lot of us, the reason we fail is because we run out of willpower. We think it's a personality fault but it's not. It's just our, and everyone else's, physiology. So if we had more willpower, or knew how to conserve it better, then we'd be able to persevere with our goals and actually fulfil them.

However, this can be very difficult when we look at the

causes of ego-depletion. It seems like those causes are very prevalent in our lives. So where does this leave us? Well, I'm going to show you why we really need to drop our old ways, and how 1-Minute Habits truly revolve around our brains' limitations and conserve our willpower better than any other strategy.

We're going to look at Big Goals and 1-Minute Habits again. But this time, I will go through the 6 causes of ego-depletion and show you the effect big goals and 1-Minute Habits have on them.

Decision Fatigue

Big Goals: With abstract goals, there is a lot of separation and disconnection with them. We then have to find ways to connect to them which involve making more decisions, such as finding ways to motivate ourselves, or deciding what to focus on every day. So our brains have to undergo a needless decision-making process.

Big goals rely on motivation, and on some days we will feel less motivated to work on them than others. This means that the decision fatigue we experience will fluctuate. So we experience needless decision-fatigue from having to figure out what to do, and from having to *constantly* motivate ourselves. And the less motivated we feel, then the more decision-fatigue we'll experience, and so the more our willpower will be drained. This is hardly optimal.

1-Minute Habits: They require a simple decision that is constant. A decision that is present-focused and process-oriented, instead of abstract. A decision that is small and takes a minute or less to do, which requires little to no motivation. So decision-fatigue is minimised.

Effort

Big Goals: A reason for so much inconsistency when it comes to big goals is that they require a lot of effort to start. The action that they entail also involves high effort. All this requires high mental processing and thus depletes willpower.

Even just thinking that something will require high effort will deplete our willpower as well, according to Karl Weick's previously mentioned study and the meta-analysis on ego-depletion. So big goals can deplete our willpower when we're not even working on them!

1-Minute Habits: They clearly require minimal effort to start. 1-Minute Habits put you on the path of least resistance and so minimise the effort involved in the actual task as well.

When it comes to over-performing, you can do as much or as little as you want once you've met the 1-Minute quota. So you can choose to act in accordance with how much energy (willpower) you have.

This flexibility helps you to conserve your energy efficiently. 1-Minute Habits also don't wastefully deplete your willpower just from thinking about doing them. The effects of effort, then, are also minimised.

Perceived Difficulty

Big Goals: The abstraction and disconnection with our goals due to them being a faraway future hope makes us perceive them to be difficult, because if they weren't difficult, then we would have already achieved them.

The mentality of having to go all in if we want to be successful also makes the tasks and our goals seem more difficult than they may be.

All this culminates in higher perceived difficulty. This makes us linger on how much effort they involve, which leads to procrastination and willpower depletion.

1-Minute Habits: Perceived difficulty is at the lowest level it can be with 1-Minute Habits. Their design promotes simplicity and ease, so they will always be effortless and lacking any perceived difficulty. Even over-performing will have low perceived difficulty. You will always only require yourself to meet the 1-Minute quota, and can over-perform afterwards. So when you begin over-performing you will have got yourself out of your comfort zone already from performing the 1-Minute Habit. You will therefore already be in motion, and will have some momentum and small wins by your side.

Having already started (which in old strategies takes a lot of effort to do) and built momentum minimises the perceived difficulty of over-performing. And small wins make us feel like our big achievements are within reach by giving us a taste of success which further reduces perceived difficulty. So, again, 1-Minute Habits also minimise this cause of ego-depletion.

Negative Affect

Big Goals: Expecting too much from ourselves and being in a continuous cycle of failure induces a lot of stress. It also makes us feel guilty and inadequate for falling short of our goal. All these induce negative affects. Big goals also put our minds in suspense. There is a vast disconnection between us and the future, so when we focus on it, it is filled with uncertainty and so we put ourselves in a state of anxiety.

This uncertainty also leads to fear. In her book *This Year I Will...* MJ Ryan states that, from initiating changes and getting out of our comfort zones, we activate fear in our brains. Fear feeds off of the uncertainty and disconnection, making you more anxious and putting you in a negative, self-fulfilling cycle, leading to further and further depletion of your willpower.

1-Minute Habits: They are stress-free. There is no guilt or shame or inadequacy with 1-Minute Habits. Their small and easy nature guarantees progress, and by over-performing, you can progress even more. Either way, you will be achieving small wins and momentum that builds into a positive feedback loop. These small wins actually serve as a source of motivation - thanks to the positive feedback loop and the prospect of increasing your streak every day. So 1-Minute Habits minimise this as well, and, if anything, induce positive affects!

Subjective Fatigue

Big Goals: When it comes to *subjective* fatigue, this is based on how tired we *personally* feel. And if there is a task that we feel is embroiled in lots of effort, difficulty, and stress, then we are going to subjectively not want to do it. Studies show that our brains make us feel more tired than we really are.[27] And this isn't confined to our regular muscles. It is also the same with our willpower muscle.[28] So if a task just doesn't look appealing, our brains will make us feel more subjectively fatigued so that we can avoid it. So, again, our old ways perpetuate willpower depletion.

Not only this, but we all tend to have a negativity bias. According to the study 'Bad is stronger than good'[29] by Baumeister: negative experiences have more of an impact on us than good ones; our brains process bad information more thoroughly than good (which partly explains why major news stories focus on negative occurrences); and we are much more biased to avoid negative-feeling experiences than to pursue positive-feeling experiences.

Furthermore, in the bestseller *Thinking, Fast and Slow*,

psychologist and Nobel Laureate Daniel Kahneman explained that we are wired to be risk-averse. We are almost twice as sensitive to potential losses (or what we think might be a loss, such as discomfort) than potential gains.

What all this means is that our minds will try their best to avoid tasks they don't like. Not only do we feel more tired than we really are, but we see uncomfortable tasks as a lot worse than they really are as well. Our minds cling onto the negative feelings we think we'll feel from those tasks. And the more we think about doing an unpleasant task, the more opportunity we give these negative voices to fill our heads and convince us not to act.

For people focused on a big goals approach, the effort, perceived difficulty, subjective fatigue, and negative affects feel a lot worse than they actually are. And if those feelings seem a lot worse, then their effects on willpower depletion will actually be even more pronounced!

1-Minute Habits: Since 1-Minute Habits aren't straining or burdening, there will be nothing for our subjective fatigue and negativity bias to cling onto. Your subjective fatigue will only be based on factors outside of 1-Minute Habits. Therefore, 1-Minute Habits minimise the effects of subjective fatigue. And subjectively, we will feel embarrassed and silly not to do them so we may even feel invigorated to fulfil our quota.

Blood Glucose

Big Goals: They require more energy, and the more energy that is used, the more blood glucose we lose. So high effort tasks sap our blood glucose which, in turn, reduces our willpower further.

1-Minute Habits: They conserve our blood glucose in the most efficient manner since they require minimal energy to perform. Therefore the effect of 1-Minute Habits on blood glucose is also minimal.

***

Phew. So I've gone on quite a crusade throughout this book to show you all the reasons why our old ways don't work. And now we can understand why. They simply don't take into account the brain's design and limitations at all. They rely on inconsistent motivation but then when that runs out, we feel overwhelmed by our high expectations and eventually give up on our goals. They don't take into account the importance of habits, and how the brain forms them. They don't take into account that, to form the habits we want, we have to align our automating basal ganglia with our pre-frontal cortices' wants. And they do not take into account how our willpower and energy is limited and what limits it.

Ego-depletion is what limits it. And big goals are filled to the brim with ego-depletion. Big goals are completely enshrouded in it. They needlessly deplete and minimise our willpower. It's no wonder we all wish for more willpower whilst we are using the usual strategies. The usual strategies squander our willpower. They deplete our willpower even before we start working on them, and they minimise it whilst working on them. They put us in a negative feedback loop that gradually and needlessly reduces our willpower more and more, until we burnout and give up.

Without a doubt, our usual approach, focusing on future Big Goals, is extremely *wasteful* for us. They do a horrible job in conserving our willpower, and leave us feeling overwhelmed and guilty. They don't take into account the limitations of the brain, and don't revolve around its design. If anything, it seems like big goals do everything that's against how our brains actually work! So it's no wonder that their failure rate is so high.

64

4.4. 1-Minute Habits Optimise the Brain

In clear and stark contrast to big goals, 1-Minute Habits minimise ego-depletion. It should be clear now to see that 1-Minute Habits use the key findings of scientific research and revolve around the limitations of our brain to get the most out of it. They facilitate repetition and consistency - the key ingredients for success and exactly what we need to align our basal ganglia with our pre-frontal cortex. They also get us out of our comfort zones constantly to familiarise us with what's outside of them so that we can grow. It builds self-confidence and makes achieving lasting change a possibility. It removes the barriers to starting. It is a system filled with flexibility so that you can progress as much or as little as you can, whilst guaranteeing progress. No other system guarantees progress like this.

1-Minute Habits work *with* the brain rather than *against* it. No other system conserves our willpower and minimises the effects of ego-depletion as much as this system. It essentially alleviates all the problems we face from our usual strategies. And by conserving willpower so effectively, it saves us energy that we can then use on over-performing. So it perpetuates a positive feedback loop that only grows stronger the more it is used.

A survey by the American Psychological Association found that people reported a 'lack of willpower' as the main reason why they couldn't achieve their goals and resolutions.[30] And according to numerous studies, our level of willpower correlates with our success.

Those who can conserve their willpower are happier, healthier, have better relationships, achieve higher grades, and are more successful in their careers and goals.[31] A meta-analysis on willpower and health found that higher willpower leads to a longer life.[32] Willpower is a better indicator of academic success than IQ.[33]

And a long-term study that tracked individuals from birth to age thirty-two found that the individuals with high self-control from a young age were physically and mentally healthier, had less criminal convictions and greater financial independence.[34] I could go on and cite many more studies but you get the point.

People with the best self-control have a higher chance of achieving what they want than people with bad self-control. And people with the best self-control are those who structure their lives so as to conserve willpower. Our big goals diminish our willpower wastefully. But 1-Minute Habits conserve our willpower optimally.

Therefore, **1-Minute Habits well and truly optimise the brain, and are conducive to success.**

We should now have a better understanding of all the benefits 1-Minute Habits bring and why we should form them. We have learnt throughout the book that our usual approach goes against our brain, and goes against science, so it should be clear now why the big goals method doesn't work.

With all this knowledge and affirmation of 1-Minute Habits and their optimisation of our brain, we can now start applying them into our lives. The next chapter will show you the simple steps we can take to implement the system.

4.5. Chapter 4 Key Facts

- Small wins are scientifically proven to be more effective and efficient compared to big wins. 1-Minute Habits embody small wins.
- 1-Minute Habits provide a reciprocal positive feedback loop.
- 1-Minute Habits reinforce starting, getting out of your comfort zone, motivation, and the belief that it's possible. All this promotes consistency.
- Big Goals are pretty much conjoined with ego-depletion. Willpower is immensely wasted.
- Success depends on willpower.
- 1-Minute Habits optimise willpower, and optimise the brain.

Part 2:
HOW

Chapter 5: Applying 1-Minute Habits

Knowing is not enough; we must apply. Willing is not enough; we must do.
- Johann Wolfgang von Goethe

5.1. The 1-Minute Habits System in 4 Simple Steps

Now we are well-equipped and knowledgeable enough to start implementing the 1-Minute Habits System. Here's how.

There are 4 simple steps:

1) **Define**
2) **Cue set-up**
3) **Chains Tracking**
4) **1-Minute Habit**

I will go through each step and provide descriptions of what they entail and give you some answers to frequently asked questions related to them. I've gone into a good amount of detail in answering any questions that you may have when applying them. But don't be put off by the detail. The detail is there for _**reference**_ in case you ever need relevant answers.

When actually applying the steps, it is much simpler. At the _end_ of this chapter I will concisely show you how to easily apply the system with a practical set of instructions. So if you find any of this chapter's FAQs aren't applicable to you, feel free to skim or skip them.

How many 1-Minute Habits should I form at once?

The recommended amount of 1-Minute Habits you should have at any time is between 1 and 4. Have too many and your attention will be divided amongst them, thereby reducing your chances to over-perform. And having too many can also lead to some ego-depletion since it can become burdensome having to juggle so many. So keep it between 1 and 4 to be safe so that you'll get all the benefits of the system. The less you have, then, the more priority you can give them.

5.2. Step 1) Define - Visualise and Simplify

Defining your 1-Minute Habit involves *Visualising* and *Simplifying* what you want to do.

When you **Visualise** you will be thinking about your long-term goal(s). I know I have said not to focus on long-term goals, but we still need them to give us a sense of direction on where to go. For the 1st part of this step, you will be visualising your goal. You will form a mental picture of your goal. You can do this by asking yourself the following simple questions: What is a goal you want to achieve? What accomplishment do you think will give you the most fulfilment?

By Visualising, you will get to see the bigger picture and get an idea of where exactly you want to be. Also by visualising and seeing what comes into your mind, you will get to see what goals you want to prioritise.

Once you have visualised what you want, you then determine what action it will take to get you to it. This is done through 2 rounds of **simplification**.

Simplify Round 1: Simplify the goal into a habit. Ask

yourself, "What core consistent action (habit) will it take to reach that goal? What can I do on a consistent basis?" Examples: If your vision is to lose lots of weight, a consistent action would be to exercise, or eat healthier food. If your vision is to become a singer, then a consistent action would be to sing.

Simplify Round 2: Then you simplify even further to something that can be done in a minute or less. You will be scaling down the core consistent action required to achieve your goal into a ridiculously easy action. This is to counter the 6 ego-depletion causes and to minimise the resistance to *start*. You want to align your 1-Minute Habit with the path of least resistance. So you must scale your habit down. You will make it something effortless, easy, and simple, something you can do in a minute or less; something that seems so small that it's laughable. The smaller the requirement, the better! You should revolve it around how you feel at your lowest: your lowest mood, and lowest level of energy. How do you feel at these points? What small actions are you capable of easily doing at these points?

To get the most out of this system you have to make your 1-Minute Habit the smallest habit initiator you can, and you must make it something that the *worst* feeling version of yourself can easily do every day.

Examples: If my vision was to be good at playing guitar, my simplification R1 could be to learn/play guitar consistently. Then the simplification R2 to make it a 1-Minute Habit could be to play guitar for a minute. Also, it can be quantity based, and not time limit based. It just has to be something really, really simple that, when multiplied, will lead to what you want. Something typically done within a minute. So it could also be play 1 short song, or chord. Or read one page of a how-to-play-guitar book.

Another example is losing weight. My Simplification R1 would be to go running. Then a Simplification R2 would be to walk outside for 1-Minute.

Define FAQ

How simple should my 1-Minute Habit be?

There is no such thing as too simple. The simpler and smaller your 1-Minute Habit, the better it will be. Remember: We want to minimise ego-depletion as much as possible and minimise all of its main causes. We want to do this to maximise the conservation of our willpower, so that we can be consistent and over-perform if we want to. So if your 1-Minute Habit requirement is so small that it's embarrassing then GREAT! That's what it should be like.

If you're ever feeling resistance in doing your 1-Minute Habit then it will mainly be because you haven't simplified it enough. The rule of thumb is that the least motivated and most tired version of yourself should be able to do your 1-Minute Habit with ease, consistently. Keep that in mind when simplifying. DO NOT let your ego or pride make you think you should have a higher quota. Yes, we all could do more, and I really want you to do more as well, but save this energy and willpower for your over-performance! I can't stress this enough. The whole point of this book is to get you to MINIMISE ego-depletion and make you CONSISTENTLY START. And you reduce your chances of doing that if you make your requirement bigger. You'll be making the whole system redundant for yourself and reducing its benefits. Avoid this at all costs. You can do as much as you want when you over-perform so keep your 1-Minute quota ridiculously easy and simple. Please remember that.

Experiment to get your 1-Minute Habit(s) correctly defined

In the beginning you may even have to experiment a tiny

amount to determine what minimises ego-depletion, and maximises consistency. Since this may all be new to you, your 1-Minute Habits might not be scaled down enough, or you might be adopting too many at once when you first start out. Look at these 2 factors and iterate accordingly. Only have 1-4 1-Minute Habits at a given time. The more 1-Minute Habits you have, the less minimised ego-depletion will be, and the less chance you give yourself to over-perform.

If you are worried that your defined 1-Minute Habit won't be optimal, don't worry. First, make sure it is scaled down enough so that even your worst version can perform it with ease. Then just try it out. Experiment with your defined 1-Minute Habit for a couple of days and see if you can maintain consistency. If you are struggling with the consistency you'll need to simplify it further. If you can over-perform with it, then that's more of a sign that it's well defined. But if you can't over-perform straight away, don't worry (more on over-performance in Step 4). It will happen eventually. Just try it out to see if you can maintain consistency.

In some cases where you want to achieve a goal/form a habit, you might have very little idea of how to go about achieving it. In this case, experiment some more. For example: You could simply turn your 1-Minute Habit into a 1-Minute Research Habit to figure out the good, easy action you can do repeatedly.

Prioritising Habits

In other cases you will have a very good idea on what you want to do. There might be a goal or habit that you want to focus on and prioritise over others. But you may also like to form 1 or 2 less prioritised 1-Minute Habits. In this case, you may find that you are consistent with and over-perform more with your prioritised habit than the others. And this is perfectly fine. You can mix and match in a sense. Have a priority 1-Minute Habit that you want to turn into a habit, so that you will try to over-perform with it whenever possible. And have other lower priority 1-Minute Habits which you can focus on simply by building their foundation and not over-performing with them much or at all.

Bear in mind that, the less 1-Minute Habits you have, and the more prioritisation you give to a specific 1-Minute Habit, then the likelier you are to over-perform and progress with it.

Concrete Definition vs. Broad Definition

Some goals, like wanting to read more books, can be easily defined into a 1-Minute Habit. A goal of wanting to read books would have the habit of reading books, and the 1-Minute Habit can be 1-Minute Reading, or read 1 paragraph. This is a *concrete definition* and doesn't really need to ever change. But then there's more progressive habits. For example, if I had a goal of, say, being good at guitar, and my habit was playing guitar - that's a bit more complex and has more stages than the reading books habit.

A concrete definition for progressive habits like playing guitar can also be easily defined and are viable. For instance, 1-Minute Practicing Guitar would be a core action. However, what can we do if we want to do something related to our goal that's outside of our concrete definition? So with the guitar example, what happens if we want to learn from a book about guitar or watch a tutorial about it to learn how to play different songs?

For this, you could create a *temporary* 1-Minute Habit, such as 1-Minute Guitar Research. Or to get more precise (which will make it easier to focus), read 1 page of a guitar book or watch a guitar tutorial for a minute. So for a day you could have your quota of 1-Minute Guitar Practice, and add 1-Minute Guitar Research that you have to also reach. The total 1-Minute Habits for that day will be 2. Eventually you may stop needing to research and so can drop the temporary 1-Minute Habit and so continue doing the 1-Minute Practicing Guitar. Then, at another point in time you might want to bring it back or even form a different temporary 1-Minute Habit that's relevant for progress. So you can add or discard temporary 1-Minute Habits at your pleasure, but you are remaining consistent with, and doing every day, your core, concretely defined 1-Minute Habit.

Instead of a concrete definition, you could make it a *broad definition*. So for a playing guitar habit, you could have a broad definition like 1-Minute Guitar. This can encompass anything you do that gets you closer to being better at it. So doing *either* 1-Minute Guitar Practice or 1-Minute Guitar Research on a day will count as that day's quota done for your 1-Minute Guitar Habit. So doing anything more with *these* habits will be over-performance. Your total 1-Minute Habits in this case will be 1.

There are advantages and disadvantages for each type of definition. For concrete definitions, the definitions are more precise. And the more 1-Minute Habit quotas you have (up to a certain point) for 1 goal, then the faster you'll progress with that goal. So for the goal of being good at guitar, you're likelier to progress quicker by having both the quotas of 1-Minute Guitar Practice AND 1-Minute Guitar Research than if you only had a quota of just practicing OR researching. But, you will have 2 quotas for the day, meaning that it leaves less room open to form other 1-Minute Habits for other goals. And you will have less flexibility with what can fulfil your quotas.

On the other hand, broader definitions give you more flexibility with what will fulfil your 1-Minute quota. The more complex and progressive the habit, then the more useful this can be. It also allows more room to form other 1-Minute Habits for other goals. The downside is that there may be less precision, so you'll have to know beforehand what exactly you can do to increase your 1-Minute Habit quota.

You could also have a mixture of the 2. Make it concrete

enough so that it's actionable, but broad enough so that it can encompass a lot of actions that are beneficial and relevant to your goal. The concrete definition above of reading books is actionable, but you could argue that it is also broad as it encompasses any book. It could be even broader by being defined as just reading, but then this might seem too broad and so won't be targeting the goal effectively. I prefer having a mixture of the 2, but you might prefer otherwise.

Either way, when defining and simplifying your habit, go with whatever definition you come up with, and then see if it works out. You don't have to decide on the outset if you're 1-Minute Habit is concrete or broad or a mixture. This sub-section is just to show you some options to consider that can make it easier for you to come up with an optimal 1-Minute Habit.

Non-Daily 1-Minute Habits and Substitute 1-Minute Habits

There may be some 1-Minute Habits that you don't want to do every day of the week, like going to the gym. To keep some sort of consistency going every day, you could have a relevant substitute 1-Minute Habit that you can do in place of your actual 1-Minute Habit. This way, on days where you can't do your 1-Minute Habit of going to the gym (due to rest days, or unable to get there days - try not to make a habit of this!), you could do related 1-Minute Habits depending on your goals. So substitute 1-Minute Habits like 1-Minute Cardio, or 1-Minute Push-ups. Try to define any substitute 1-Minute Habits beforehand, because it may seem like cheating if you decide to do the substitute in place of the core 1-Minute Habit when you weren't planning to.

Defining Tricky 1-Minute Habits like Going to the Gym

Also, this is a good opportunity to go into more detail

about 1-Minute Habits like going to the gym. There may be some habits that you want to form which seem quite tricky to simplify and define. But it can be done. You just have to get a little creative. I mentioned that 1-Minute Habits are a sort of habit initiator. So just bear that in mind and figure out what action initiates you to go to the gym. Examples include: putting on your gym clothes or driving there. So you could essentially have a 1-Minute Habit of getting ready for the gym, or a 1-Minute driving to the gym habit. They are habit initiators and are getting you in motion to workout at the gym, so you can use 1-Minute Habits like them. It probably will take you longer than 1 minute to get ready, or drive there, but the 1-Minute Habits themselves are within a minute and are getting you to move towards doing what you really want.

You can simplify just about any action you want to do, and turn it into a 1-Minute Habit. And you can simplify 1-Minute Habits themselves, as we just saw, where the 1-Minute Gym Habit, can turn into a 1-Minute drive to the gym habit. We could even simplify that further and say a 1-Minute getting into the car habit. The latter is still initiating you to act. Whatever is simple, whatever has the least resistance, and whatever gets you to act accordingly with your goals and habits, do that for your 1-Minute Habit.

The reason you'd want to simplify a 1-Minute Habit of visiting the gym further is due to relativity. Your 1-Minute Habits are subject to the habit that you want to form. So the 1-Minute Habit of going to the gym might be more strenuous than say the 1-Minute Habit of writing. Or the 1-Minute Habit of exercise will be a bit more uncomfortable depending on your fitness levels. It's all relative to the habit. So, since putting on your gym clothes and driving to the gym get you to start your gym habit, they can be classified as part of your 1-Minute Gym Habit.

As I've said, the 1-Minute Habits System is filled with flexibility. Also remember: you don't have to be confined to the time element of 1-Minute. You can also use quantity.

If it is still too difficult for you to maintain consistency with something like a gym habit, then you will have to simplify it even more. Find what is giving you resistance and then make your 1-Minute Habit minimise that specific resistance. The resistance may stem from the traveling, or social anxiety, or fitness levels. Either way, you can find a solution. A solution for all these forms of resistances would be to just have a 1-Minute Habit that you can do at home or somewhere closer to home. There are countless free exercise tutorials available on the web so you could start off with working out at home with, say, a 1-Minute Push-up Habit, and then, over time, once there isn't resistance for you to work out, going to the gym should be much easier.

Disclaimer: All the examples I've used so far are not exclusive. The context of the examples can be applied to many, many other habits. I've just used habits such as a gym habit, because they are quite popular and so would be easier to understand.

Now let's look at Step 2.

5.3. Step 2) Cue set-up

The main cue that we want to set-up is simply the cue that will remind us what time we should do our 1-Minute Habit. This is called the when-cue.

When-cue

This cue is simply deciding how you will fit 1-Minute

Habits into your schedule and at what specific point during the day you will do them. You can choose 1 of 3 approaches to form this cue. You can choose a *Routine* approach where you will revolve your 1-Minute Habit around a specific time and/or around a certain action (e.g. before work, after dinner). For example, a routine when-cue could be, 'Do my 1-Minute Exercise Habit at 6pm', which is time based, or 'Do my 1-Minute Studying Habit before Dinner' which is action based. You could also have a mixture of the time and action, like 'After Work, Before 8pm'. These time and action based cues can be inflexible though, but are good if you have a strict schedule and can stick to routine.

Or you can opt for an *Open* approach where you do it whenever you feel like doing it or whenever you can during the day. This is good if you don't have a strict schedule. You won't be relying on a certain time and action to do it which makes it more flexible.

Depending on your daily routine, choose whichever one is most viable for you. Or use a *Mixed* approach - a combination of the two. So choose to do your 1-Minute Habit of exercising in the morning, however, if that doesn't work out, do it whenever you are free during the rest of the day. But don't make a habit of wanting to do it at a certain time then ending up doing it at another. Just do this as a sort of contingency plan.

Since they are 1-Minute Habits, they will be able to fit into your lifestyle regardless of your routine and what you do. However, just keep in mind that the more flexible your routine is, the likelier you are to over-perform as you'll be able to set aside more time to do so.

***

There are also two other cues you could add to your arsenal. These cues can benefit you, but aren't mandatory to get the full benefits of the system. They are just an extra perk you can add if your circumstances need them. These are *Positive* and *Negative* cues. They provide a way to look out for your future-self by making it easier or harder for them to do certain actions. This is because the future is uncertain and we can't always trust ourselves to do the actions we plan to do when the time comes.

Positive and negative cues involve putting things into place that decrease the decision-making process for positive actions, and increase the decision-making process for negative actions, respectively. Positive cues aim to facilitate positivity; negative cues aim to obstruct negativity. So these 2 types of cues are good for those who have a lot of temptations and distractions in their lives that they'd like to weaken.

Positive cue

The positive cues assist you in doing your 1-Minute Habit. Now, you might think that this isn't necessary since 1-Minute Habits are so easy and don't emit any resistance. But if you have consistent trouble in over-performing AND would like to over-perform, then setting up positive cues can help to facilitate it by making it even *easier* to start.

Examples of positive cues include setting reminders, or setting alarms. Or, say, if you had a 1-Minute Habit of writing, a positive cue in this case could be to lay out your notepad and pen beforehand, or could be to put your laptop in noticeable location beforehand. If you had a 1-Minute Habit of walking outside, then a positive cue could be having your exercise clothes set out and easily noticeable.

You see, positive cues are simply reducing the decision-making process for positive actions. Having them isn't mandatory to get the full benefits of the system, but it is an option for you to consider if you want a little more convenience for certain 1-Minute

Habits, and/or if you want to make over-performing easier by making it more convenient to start and get momentum going.

Negative cue

Negative cues make it a bit harder to do negative actions by increasing the decision-making process and reducing convenience. These can be used for breaking bad habits if you go down that route. But since the system is focused on forming good habits, you can instead use negative cues to diminish the effect of temptations and distractions in your life that may get in your way. By making it harder to do negative habits, you again may increase the chances of over-performing as it may free up some time that otherwise would've been spent being distracted.

An example of setting up a negative cue: If you feel you procrastinate a lot and get distracted by, say, video games and want to focus on other things, simply increase the decision-making process involved with starting to play video games. So when your energy is high, make yourself take the wires and plugs out of your console, or move your controller to another room. This way, when your energy is low later on, and you are more susceptible to distractions you will have made it less convenient to start indulging. Each negative cue (putting wires back in, moving controller back to play) serves as a reminder that you shouldn't be playing them at this moment. It *disrupts the automaticity* of bad habits, thereby giving you a greater chance to consciously step in and stop yourself from giving in.

Another simple example: You want to lose weight, but in your house there are a lot of delicious unhealthy snacks which you give into when your willpower is low. So when your energy is high, make yourself simply increase the decision-making process involved in getting these snacks. Move them to a harder to reach place (and you could also move healthy snacks into a more convenient place). Again, this will disrupt the automaticity of your bad habit.

These negative cues may sound a bit silly, but if you have a lot of trouble controlling your impulses, they are a powerful tool at your disposal which may help. They simply increase inconvenience for bad habits. They're not about abstinence or suppression, they are just a way to remind you of your goals, and keep you focused on them.

***

Positive and negative cues prevent you from becoming automated into doing things that take you away from your goals. Each positive and negative cue will serve as a reminder, and when your brain reacts to the cue, it will remember that there was a reason it set those cues up in the first place (for your goals, habits, and 1-Minute Habits), and so it will increase your chances of initiating positive behaviours and avoiding negative behaviours.

I want to reiterate though, that setting up positive cues and negative cues is not mandatory. But if you feel they can help you, then by all means, go for it. To some, positive and negative cues may help with convenience; to others they may seem burdensome. Add them or don't, depending on what you think is best.

The when-cue is important though, so make sure you set that one up to make it convenient for you to fit your 1-Minute Habit(s) into your schedule.

5.4. Step 3) Chains Tracking

One of the greatest techniques I have come across during my research is *Chains Tracking*. Jerry Seinfeld - the richest actor and comedian in the world[35] - brought to light this method.[36] What is this chains technique? Well, Jerry Seinfeld understood that to succeed and excel at anything in life requires incremental daily progress. He knew that, if he wanted to be a successful comedian, he would have to work on his jokes every single day. Jerry Seinfeld is a sure as can be real life example of how systems like 1-Minute Habits are keys to success.

He knew he had to be consistent if he wanted to be successful. He knew he had to write every day. But he also understood that writing every day can seem daunting and would require constant motivation. He knew that, if he didn't write and work on what mattered on one day, it would be likely that he wouldn't work the next day, and so on. To maintain consistency, he used an extremely simple calendar system which I wholeheartedly recommend you also adopt. He had a giant wall calendar which shows the whole year on one page, and hung it up on a wall so that he'd be forced to notice it. Everyday where he'd write jokes he would get a red marker and place a big, fulfilling X over that day. Writing jokes one day made it easier for him to write on the next day and so on. Remember this: What you do today will likely be what you do tomorrow. And so after a few days of writing jokes consecutively, he'd have a row of Xs. He'd have a chain. A streak. Whatever you want to call it. He had built consistency, and built momentum and was on a roll.

Sticking with his daily habit of writing jokes meant that his chain grew larger and larger. Eventually he had concocted a large chain of Xs that would make him feel proud to look at. Each X he would draw resulted in a *small win*. As you know, small wins lead to momentum, and a positive cycle ensues. And he would want to maintain consistency otherwise he'd '*break the chain*'.

So for you, on days where you don't feel good, having built up a chain will urge you into action because you won't want to break your chain. This will help you in maintaining consistency.

One way you might end up breaking your chain is if the task you have set yourself is too much for you to handle. But with 1-Minute Habits that will never be the case, as long as you clearly define your habit to be ridiculously simple and don't try to form too many at once.

The 1-Minute Habits System is a strong advocate of this technique because, at its core, this technique helps you do exactly what this book is for - it helps you become consistent. It all culminates in helping you develop consistency in an action that will build a foundation of positive change. The idea of tracking and reaching personal records (such as a chain of 100 days) is motivating and positively affirming. It can add a disruption in your impulses of doing opposing things because you will remind yourself that your chain will break.

Jerry Seinfeld used a giant wall calendar for his habit of writing jokes. It might be difficult for those who adopt more than one 1-Minute Habit at a given time to have individual giant wall calendars for each. Fortunately, the chains tracking technique does not discriminate against different shapes, sizes, and types of calendars for it to work. As long we have something that can be marked for each day to show progress and show a streak then it will work. So any normal calendar will work, but there are also some alternatives that may be more convenient for you. These are: printable calendars, hand-made calendars; calendar chains software; and calendar chains phone apps.

Print and Hand-made Calendars

The good thing about a giant wall calendar is its prominent display. It is very noticeable. So if you have a smaller sized calendar, just make sure you put it in a noticeable place. At the time of writing this book, I have four A4 calendars for each of my 1-Minute Habits (meditation, exercise, reading, and writing) which

I place on my bedroom wall that's parallel to my bed. Placing them near your bed means that, if some unforeseen event occurs during the day and you haven't been able to think about your 1-Minute Habits, you are reminded about them before you sleep and can maintain consistency.

Once you've defined your 1-Minute Habit and set-up your when-cue, simply print off a free calendar from any website, such as http://www.printfree.com/Calendars.htm[37] (I found this by Googling "free calendar"). You can print off monthly or yearly calendars for each of your 1-Minute Habits. Monthly calendars are nice because your Xs will look bigger, but having 12 calendars for each 1-Minute Habit may take up too much space on your wall. And if you only print out these calendars once a month, then that can be a drag. Yearly calendars are the usual calendars used for chains tracking, and they take up less space. Choose whichever one is convenient for you.

You could also create a hand-made calendar instead. This is done by drawing a grid of any size you want on a piece of paper or card. Over on reddit.com, there is a great sub-reddit called /r/thexeffect. This is a community of people using the chains technique for their personal development. How they track their chains is via Hand-made Calendars and you can apply 1-Minute Habits to their steps. You simply get a piece of paper or card and draw a 5x10, 10x5 or 7x7 +1 grid, so that you'll have 50 squares. 50 days is a nice number as it is large but not excessively so. Once you meet your 1-Minute quota, you then draw an X on your card and increase your chain for that day.

How long should my chain be?

This is basically the same as asking how long it takes to form a habit. An **important** thing to mention with this, and with 1-Minute Habits in general, is that, once you reach a designated number like a 50 day streak, that doesn't mean you'll have the habit and now you won't need to do it ever again. The point of 50 is that, if you can do 50, then doing 60 won't be as difficult. If you can do 60 then getting to 80 won't be as hard. And so on, until the habit truly becomes automated. Once it's automated, it will be internalised, and so you can improve on it further, or form another 1-Minute Habit. You see, 1-Minute Habits aim to give you progress and benefits for as long as possible. So your chain shouldn't really have a limit. And since the time it takes to form a habit is uncertain, there is no definitive number on how long your chain should be.

Chains Applications

Technology is such a big part of our lives that it's a good idea to use our computers and/or our phones to help track our progress too.

Since 1-Minute Habits are meant to be simple and straightforward, the only way we can really 'break our chains' (ruin our streak) is if we somehow forget to work on them. But this shouldn't really occur either since 1-Minute Habits are for our goals and therefore should be a prioritised thought. However, there may be days where you become so occupied with other responsibilities, or unforeseen events that you may not think about your 1-Minute Habits. Unlikely, but it could happen. That's why I advise on keeping your calendars up on walls in your bedroom so that they're in plain sight. But since we won't always be at home, it is wise and extremely convenient to have a chains tracking app with us on our smartphones.

My favourite chains tracking application is Chains.cc.[38] It's quite different from other chains apps because it shows your chain vertically instead of in a calendar grid. But that is part of its charm. It is a great, colourful, beautifully designed chains tracker that is free to use on computers, and is accessed via browsers, so no download is required. It's also available for download on iOS devices for £1.49/$1.99. I have an Android phone so I can't download the app on there, but you can still access the website of it on your Android phone's browsers. It then provides a simplified mobile interface that is similar to the iOS version (and is free).

Other great chains tracking apps are: Lift (free for iOS & Android); and MyChain (free and only for Android). All these apps allow us to input the 1-Minute Habits we want to form and record their progress daily. There are a few variations amongst them though. Chains.cc is visually appealing and has a minimalist design. Lift isn't as visually appealing but it gets the job done. A word of caution though is that Lift may give you recommendations of habits. These do not give the benefits of 1-Minute Habits so just ignore them and input your defined 1-Minute Habits. MyChain is also very simple and minimalist but its interface and design are lacking. But it is great because it gives you the option of widgets. You can place a counter on your phone's screen, and when you do your 1-Minute Habit you can touch the counter and it goes up by 1 for the day - a pretty awesome and intuitive way to increase your chain. And you can place this widget on your home screen which is a prominent location and so will serve as a good way to remind you to do your 1-Minute Habits.

Wall calendars, printable calendars, hand-made calendars, computer and phone apps - there's a vast selection to choose from. Pick whatever methods suit you best. The good thing about the wall, printable, or hand-made ones - the *analogue* chain trackers - is that they require you to physically record each increase in your streak, so they reinforce your 1-Minute Habit both visually and kinetically. For me, the satisfaction of physically drawing an X feels greater than clicking or tapping the chain on my computer or phone. Not only that but experiments show that writing things down makes them have a greater presence in our memories and so will be easier to remember.[39] Keeping this in mind, I also recommend you write down your definition and cue set-up.

It is unclear whether tapping or typing has the same effect as writing. Therefore using analogue chains trackers may make your 1-Minute Habits easier to remember than using apps. But since we live in the digital age, I recommend using a phone app too, so you can track your progress on the go.

Chains Tracking provides numerous benefits

Helping you remember to do your 1-Minute Habits is far from the only reason for using this technique. We know about the positive feedback loop of small wins 1-Minute Habits provide. Well, chains tracking reinforces that positive feedback loop even more! By increasing your chain, recording it, and setting personal records, you will be achieving another small win. You will also feel a sense of satisfaction from looking at your streak and will want to increase it more. The idea of your chain breaking will be something you want to avoid, so you will be even *more* motivated to do your 1-Minute Habits. They will also serve as a positive cue as when you see them, you will be reminded to do your 1-Minute Habit. Chains tracking pushes you to be consistent and, with 1-Minute Habits already revolving around consistency, this whole system minimises the chance of inconsistency as much as is possible. Therefore, it coincides with success.

Chains Tracking for Non-Daily 1-Minute Habits

As stated in *Step 1) Define*, there may be some 1-Minute Habits that you don't want to do every day of the week, such as going to the gym. Chains Tracking in this case can involve two options. 1) You can simply make a note on your calendars or change the settings on your chains apps that you will only do your 1-Minute Habit on those specific days and then leave the off-days blank and continue as normal (this is if you don't have a substitute habit); or 2) If you have a relevant substitute 1-Minute Habit you can make a note on your calendars of the days where you will do these substitutes, such as by putting a / or \ instead of a full X, or an S for substitute. Whatever you want. You could also just create a separate calendar for the substitute 1-Minute Habit.

Breaking your chain

Breaking your chain means that you weren't able to perform your 1-Minute Habit consistently and missed a day. So what happens? Nothing really, except there will be a gap in your chain. Simply figure out what was the cause of this gap, and start your chain again. Starting again won't be difficult since 1-Minute Habits reduce the resistance of starting. You may feel bad for ruining your streak but it's ok. Just get back up and try to reach that personal record again, and beat it. But never ever increase your chain when you haven't done your quotas. Don't cheat!

It is unlikely for you to break your chain anyway if you apply the system correctly. So figure out where you might have gone wrong. The reasons you weren't able to maintain consistency could be:

1) Your 1-Minute Habit wasn't simplified enough and so was too strenuous. Simplify it so that the worst version of yourself could do it.

2) You might have simplified all your habits as much as is possible, but you have tried to adopt too many 1-Minute Habits at once. Cut down on how many 1-Minute Habits you have. Keep it between 1-4.

3) And although you may have applied the system correctly, there might have been a serious emergency. In this case you could put something different on your calendars in place of an X, such as an E for emergency. Or put a note in your chains app (if it allows you to) on the day.

Regardless of the reason, it doesn't matter that you broke

it. Your progress won't go anywhere. You will still have all the progress and benefits you accumulated already. Just start your chain again and restart the continuous cycle of success, so that you can maintain the neural pathways of the 1-Minute Habit and strengthen them.

5.5. Step 4) 1-Minute Habit

So, here we go... The moment of truth.

Doing your 1-Minute Habit

If you've done the previous 3 steps, then this should be a cinch. Simply do the action you have defined. The action that you may have set cues up for. The action you have created a chain for. The action that, when done consistently over time, will bring you numerous benefits.

Over-performing:

Over-performing depends on your comfort and skill level, and on how much you prioritise your goal. Building up your comfort should come first. Skill and prioritisation will come whilst you gradually accumulate small wins. But if you have skill and a priority then great, that will help you. If you don't, it doesn't matter. They will come over time.

1-Minute Habit quota

It is great to set aside time so that you can over-perform. However, although we are trying to over-perform as much as possible, we should never have the requirement or quota to do it. Over-performing is a bonus. It is an extra win. Don't try to have your quota be anything greater than 1-Minute (or greater than the simplified quantity you set that can be done within a minute). And don't try to build your quota up over time. Keep it at 1-Minute always.

Where you want to focus on doing greater and building more, is in your over-performance. Once you start expecting yourself to over-perform and sub-consciously increase your requirement from a 1-Minute Habit to something more strenuous, then you will simply be diverging towards failure. Why? Because the greater the requirement the greater the chance of ego-depletion. As you gradually build up your requirement, you will gradually build up your ego-depletion which is not conducive to success. Where 1-Minute Habits excel is in minimising ego-depletion as much as possible, so by increasing the requirement, you will be marginalising the full benefits of the 1-Minute Habits System.

So ALWAYS KEEP YOUR 1-MINUTE HABIT SMALL! Don't ever change the small requirement. You can experiment and change them to another 1-Minute Habit if the latter is more optimal, but always keep them small and ridiculously easy. And always only expect to do the 1-Minute Habit. They are your quota.

The only reason you'd want to increase your 1-Minute quota is because you think it'll help you progress quicker. Which brings me to the next sub-section.

You can progress faster (only if you can and are comfortable with doing so)

You can progress as much and as quick as you can with 1-Minute Habits. Your quota and requirement is to do your 1-Minute Habit, and do it once a day. But you can also initiate your 1-Minute Habits more than once a day, however many times you want to. This means you can progress quicker with them.

You can then also over-perform as many times as you initiate your 1-Minute Habits. And you can over-perform however long or short you want, or not at all. Of course, the more you over-perform, then the faster your progress will be. But even if you don't over-perform at all you will still be making progress with your quotas.

Regardless of your circumstances and comfort levels, you can implement 1-Minute Habits in whatever way fits you. There is immense flexibility with how much you can progress, no matter who you are. Remember: 1-Minute Habits will never hold you back from progressing as much as you can, and want to.

So keep your quota a daily 1-Minute Habit, but progress faster if you want by initiating it more than once and over-performing more than once.

Decide to over-perform only in the moment

Over-perform only when you want to, whilst IN THE MOMENT. If you want to go further with your 1-Minute Habit then that's awesome, but go further in your over-performance when IN THE MOMENT. Don't decide on any day that you are going to do more than your 1-Minute or are going to over-perform lots. Only decide to over-perform whilst doing your 1-Minute Habit or straight after - so whilst being in motion.

You want to minimise ego-depletion before working, so that you can then use your conserved willpower to over-perform. You are essentially ***doing less so you can do more***.

So plan to only do your 1-Minute Habit(s).

What to do if you want to over-perform but can't?

If you are consistently doing your 1-Minute Habit AND WANT to over-perform but are finding it very difficult to do so, then you have to look at why. One reason might be because your when-cue doesn't allow for much extra time in your schedule. In this case, you could set-up your when-cue for when you have more time to do your 1-Minute Habit, and over-perform if you want to whilst in that moment. But just because you set yourself up with more time, don't expect to do more in it. You want to keep your quota minimal.

Another reason might be because you are too distracted. In this case, look at where you are spending a lot of your time and set-up negative cues for the things you feel are disposable.

A third reason might be because you find over-performing too difficult. This might be because you have not defined your 1-Minute Habit correctly. It might not be ego-depletion proof. What I mean by that is that you probably defined it as something too strenuous, something that doesn't minimise ego-depletion as it should. Define it correctly so you can get the full benefits of the system.

If your 1-Minute Habit is defined correctly, then you could also try to set-up positive cues to increase your chances of over-performing.

What happens if you don't feel like over-performing?

However, there will, of course, be times when you don't want to over-perform and that is completely fine. The requirement, plan, and focus of 1-Minute Habits is to meet the quota of the 1-Minute Habit once a day. Stop whenever you feel like stopping. Your habit is meant to last you a long time and you want to do this for a long time, so whenever you really don't feel like over-performing, don't. Just keep going everyday with your 1-Minute Habit until it becomes easy enough to over-perform consistently.

Forming a 1-Minute Habit whilst rarely ever over-performing.

Even if you don't ever over-perform but meet your 1-Minute quotas every day then that is still damn great. You will be on your way to forming a 1-Minute Habit.

From forming a 1-Minute Habit, you will form a scaled down version of the habit that you want to form along with the habits that make up the positive feedback loop. When it comes to progressing, learning, or mastering anything, we have to start with a base, the base which consists of the fundamentals. And through forming this base is where everything else will grow. Think of it like building a house. You build a house one brick at a time. 1-Minute Habits will be that brick. Every day you do your 1-Minute Habit, you will have laid an extra brick. This extra brick makes it easier to build more. This extra brick strengthens your foundation so that laying down more bricks will become easier. As you lay more and more bricks, you will habitualise and internalise brick laying. This means that doing more complex building tasks (like over-performing) will be feasible. When you over-perform, you lay down many bricks at once, and the more you over-perform, the quicker the house will be built.

The point, though, is that, regardless of whether you over-perform or not, you will still be progressing. You will be building a habit foundation, which will make forming that habit easier over time. So if you start out with never over-performing, it doesn't matter because, eventually, when the foundation has been built, you will be able to over-perform at least a little bit. But just because you begin to/can over-perform doesn't mean that you will always do so. Like I said, the expectation and requirement is only to meet the 1-Minute Habit. Your requirement is to only lay 1 brick. But, whilst doing your 1-Minute Habit - laying that brick - you can decide right there in the moment whether or not you want to do more, and then do however much you can until you want to stop.

As long as you are consistent, you'll likely start to over-perform more often when your foundation is built. Then, as you over-perform more often, your house will get built faster and become bigger. The rate at which you progress will increase over time, making your progress perpetuate increasing progress.

Internalising your 1-Minute Habit and over-performance

Once your 1-Minute Habit is internalised, you will have not only ingrained it and made it automatic, but you will also ingrain the habits of the positive feedback loop: starting; getting out of your comfort zone; motivation; and belief that it's possible. Once these are internalised, over-performing will be even more likely.

As you over-perform more, over-performance itself will eventually become internalised and form into a habit. And once you reach that stage, the possibilities for you will be endless.

A little bit about my 1-Minute Habits and over-performance

It's probably best to round off all this talk of quotas and over-performance with how I did them with my 1-Minute Habits.

Currently, I rarely ever initiate my 1-Minute Habits more than once a day, except for my 1-Minute Writing Habit. That's because it is *currently* (at the time of writing) something I want to progress faster with than my other 1-Minute Habits. So right now it's my priority habit. Whenever I initiate my 1-Minute Meditation, Exercise, and Reading Habits, I do them, usually over-perform with them, and then leave them for the day. With my 1-Minute Writing Habit, however, I initiate it however many times I can and want to during the day, and then over-perform with it each time.

I started off with doing very little to no over-performance with all of them. Only after a few weeks did I gradually do more. And then a few weeks later (depending on the 1-Minute Habit) they became habits and so were comfortable to do and over-perform with. So I now over-perform much more often with all of them. However, how much I over-perform varies, and there are still times when I don't feel like over-performing with some of them, so then I just do their quota and that's it.

Update Chain

Once you have done your 1-Minute Habit, and may or may not have over-performed, you can then update your chain. I recommend you update it at the end of the day. This is because, if you do your 1-Minute Habit early in the morning and then update your chain, you might not feel urged to do it again and over-perform during the rest of the day.

5.6. Summary of the 4 Steps

Simplicity is the ultimate sophistication.
- Leonardo da Vinci

Here you will find a simplified version of the 1-Minute Habits System combined with the key facts of this chapter. What I've written is straightforward and actionable, so you can easily follow the steps and start applying the system.

There are two more chapters left after this one where you'll learn about some beneficial habits you should form, and examples of applying the system to popular habits, respectively. So you could finish reading them and then come back here. Or you can finish reading this and start applying the system right away. I've also put an even briefer version of these steps at the end of the book as well, so you can just keep reading on normally and then start applying them straight after finishing the book.

Step 1) Define: Visualise and Simplify

Visualise: Answer the following questions: What are your goals? What do you want to achieve? What accomplishment will give you the most fulfilment?

To answer them, take a step back from your book, close your eyes, and repeat the questions. Then visualise the answers in your head. Look at what you want to accomplish. This will help you to see what you want to prioritise.

Don't worry if you feel unsure of what you want. Just look at where you think you want to make improvements in your life. Envision that. You could also look into your past and see what goals or resolutions you've tried to achieve but couldn't, and visualise them here as well. [*But if you are still unsure because you don't really know what you want to achieve, then the next 2 chapters will be of great help.*]

You've seen the goal you want to achieve?

Now simplify it.

Simplify Round 1: What is a core action that, done repeatedly, will get you closer to that goal? Take a step back from your book, close your eyes, and repeat the question in your head. Find the answer and see it.

Got it?

Simplify Round 2: Scale that habit down so that it seems laughable. Scale it down so that the worst version of yourself can easily do it. Scale it down to an action that can be done in a minute or less - it doesn't have to be confined to a minute, it can be a quantity based action (as long as it can be done within a minute).

Congrats, you now have defined your 1-Minute Habit. This will be the action you do every day to meet your quota.

2) Cue set-up

When cue: Decide when in the day you want to do your 1-Minute Habit.

When can you do your 1-Minute Habit?

Either have a routine approach, where your 1-Minute Habit is done during a certain time or action (e.g. before 12pm, or after work) if you have a strict schedule and/or prefer routines.

Or, for more flexibility, choose an open approach where you do it whenever you can during the day, if you have a flexible schedule.

You can combine the 2 options as well.

You could also make your when-cue take into account the possibility of over-performance. DON'T expect to over-perform, but you can set aside some extra time, just in case you decide to over-perform when in the moment.

[I have omitted positive and negative cues in this section because 1) They aren't mandatory, they are extra tools that can be used to help us; 2) They depend on the habit, and depend on our personal distractions so I can't give all-encompassing positive and negative cues; And 3) I give examples of these cues in chapter 7.]

3) Chains Tracking

Record your 1-Minute Habit progress by using the chains tracking method. Buy/Print/Draw a calendar, label it with your defined 1-Minute Habit, and put it up on your wall. Then once you reach your 1-Minute quota for the day, cross the day out on the calendar and repeat the next day and so on.

You should also download a chains tracking app for your phone like Chains.cc, Lift, or MyChain, or any that you find and prefer, so you can track your daily progress on the go.

4) 1-Minute Habit

Do your 1-Minute Habit, and make sure you maintain consistency with the 1-Minute Habit quota. Whilst doing your 1-Minute Habit, you can also decide on over-performing, where you'll work on your habit for longer. Over-performing is a bonus and is not required, but is recommended for more progress.

AND THAT'S IT. Simple.

Gradually, you will accrue and accumulate all the small wins this system promotes, and you'll be in a positive feedback loop of benefits and improvements. You'll be minimising failure, optimising your brain, and will eventually form the habits you want and then achieve the goals you want.

Chapter 6: The Willpower Gym

No man is free who is not master of himself.
- Epectitus

Most powerful is he who has himself in his own power.
- Seneca

I am, indeed, a king, because I know how to rule myself.
- Pietro Aretino

6.1. Training your Willpower Muscle

So, using the 1-Minute Habits System optimises our brain and efficiently conserves our willpower - conserves being the key word here. We have looked at how there is a strength model of willpower, and understand that it is like a muscle. And like a muscle, it gets tired the more we use it. But muscles can also grow stronger, so can we strengthen our willpower?

The answer to that is a resounding yes. Like a muscle, our willpower gets drained. And like a muscle it can also be trained.

We know that optimally conserving and strengthening our willpower can change our lives for the better. It is no question, then, that training our willpower muscle can be one of the best decisions we will ever make. So what exactly trains our willpower?

Well, you'll be happy to hear that 1-Minute Habits can train it. Yes, according to the ego-depletion meta-analysis mentioned in chapter 3, any *consistent* act of self-control can train our willpower. So if 1-Minute Habits also strengthens our willpower, then with our stronger willpower we'll be even more likely to work on them, over-perform, and maintain consistency. 1-Minute Habits make doing 1-Minute Habits easier over time. So we again see another way the system amplifies its effectiveness and efficacy. The system constantly reinforces itself to make its positive feedback loop grow more and more. Like a snowball effect, the benefits of this system accumulate increasingly over time.

This sounds similar to habit-formation where automaticity conserves energy which makes doing the habit easier. However, automaticity in a habit and strengthening willpower are quite distinct. They both make it easier to do our 1-Minute Habits and over-perform over time. But by strengthening our willpower muscle, it raises our willpower reserve, and strengthens our self-control in *general*. It therefore makes it easier and likelier for us to do any other act of self-control.

1-Minute Habits are an excellent way to strengthen our willpower muscle, because they train it efficiently.

If someone goes to the gym for the first time to work out their muscles, do they go for extremely heavy weights? No. Why? Because they know that that would be extremely difficult for them and could lead to injury. You wouldn't go into a gym for the first time and bench 300kg would you?

You'd start with lighter weights. Start with weights that you feel comfortable with, and gradually work your way to using heavier weights as your strength increases. The same rules apply to willpower. But because willpower isn't tangible, we don't realise that we are lifting and straining our willpower too much.

We let our ego and pride get in the way. We wrongly yet understandably assume that willpower is infinite and requires nothing but the right state of mind. Although the right state of mind is important, it will not be enough to form the right habits if you keep employing the wrong strategy and straining yourself too much.

Again, that's why 1-Minute Habits are so conducive to success. They won't strain and overwhelm your willpower muscle.

Are there other ways to strengthen our willpower muscle? You bet! This chapter will show you a number of ways you can start strengthening your willpower.

So let's enter 'The Willpower Gym'.

6.2. Trivial Uncomfortable Actions

Well, we know the metaphorical willpower muscle can be strengthened. Any muscle increases in strength in the beginning through lifting small weights repetitively and consistently over time. If we want our biceps to get bigger, we have to perform exercises that target our biceps, and do them repetitively and consistently.

Therefore, it makes perfect sense that, for us to strengthen our willpower, we must begin by doing exercises that target and use our willpower *effectively*. Any act of *self-control* targets our willpower muscle - emphasis on the self-control. So it is not enough for your willpower to be tired or depleted. This doesn't mean your willpower was actively and effectively used.

The reason for this is that our willpower's energy source is shared by other functions of the brain. So we shouldn't assume willpower depletion means willpower training. Only when your willpower is depleted from exerting self-control does it get trained. Self-control itself is being aware of your actions and correcting them. We can strengthen it by being aware of our 'comfort', and correcting ourselves into doing a less comfortable action.

So what uncomfortable things can we do? Well, according to studies, we can strengthen our willpower via trivial uncomfortable actions - these include, working on your posture, using your non-dominant hand, uncrossing your legs, and even keeping track of your spending.[40]

It isn't the specific acts themselves that improve our willpower. It is from our brain being aware of what we are doing (such as having a slouched back), and then choosing to do the more 'difficult' and 'uncomfortable' action (improving posture). It is consciously choosing to get our brains out of their comfort zone that strengthens willpower. And from these examples, and from what we have learnt about 1-Minute Habits, we clearly see that getting out of our comfort zones doesn't have to be all that difficult or uncomfortable for us to improve our willpower.

As long as we are pausing-and-planning (more on this in next section); as long as we become *self-aware*, and then *self-regulate*. By choosing to get even a little less comfortable, we will be exerting self-control and thereby strengthening our willpower muscle. Note that it isn't about being masochistic or anything like that. It is just about getting ourselves out of our comfort zone as much as possible to get our mind used to doing difficult and uncomfortable things. It is the difficulty and discomfort of tasks that depletes our willpower a lot, so by essentially getting our brain used to discomfort is a way to strengthen our willpower and reduce ego-depletion's hold on us.

So if you want a quick exercise to strengthen willpower, simply use your non-dominant hand for things like brushing your teeth, opening doors, or correct your posture right now and keep correcting it when you find yourself slouching.

6.3. Stress Reduction, Health Improvement, and Heart Rate Variability

S tress is a normal part of life. It is our mind and body's reaction to any change that requires an adjustment or response.

Evolutionarily speaking, stress helped our ancestors to survive in emergencies.

But stress is incompatible with willpower. Why? Because our physiology when we are stressed and our physiology when we exert willpower are completely opposite. When we are stressed, our body goes into what is referred to as the *fight-or-flight* response. The pre-frontal cortex, which is in charge of impulse control and willpower, becomes hindered when it experiences this response.[41] So stress makes us more impulsive. Not only that, but too much stress brings about a number of health problems.[42] Stress is the mind and body killer.

On the other hand, when we exert willpower, our body goes into what is referred to as the *pause-and-plan* response. Just from their names, you can see how at odds the fight-or-flight and pause-and-plan responses are. These 2 responses affect both the mind and body. We speed up, are impulsive, tense, and may hyperventilate when in the fight-or-flight response. But we slow down, are calm, in control, and less impulsive when in the pause-and-plan response.

One of the best ways these responses are measured, and in turn one of the best physiological measures of willpower, is heart rate variability (HRV). Heart rate variability shouldn't be confused with the heart rate. HRV is the time interval between heartbeats, or the beat-to-beat fluctuations in the heart rate, whilst heart rate is just the speed of the heartbeat (measured in beats per minute (bpm)).

High HRV and pausing and planning go hand in hand, and promote self-control.[43] When our heartbeat intervals fluctuate, that means our heart is more active, healthier, and able to respond to changes quicker and adjust the blood flow efficiently. So in response to that, we become less impulsive and more in control.

High HRV, then, is something we should all work to attain. High HRV correlates to a healthier heart and good health in general. It reflects a flexible nervous system, stress resilience, and inner strength. Stress, however, reduces our HRV, as does being ill and unhealthy.[44]

So stress reduction, health improvements, and high HRV can conserve and strengthen our willpower.

It would be very viable, then, for us to form habits which coincide with these benefits.

What are these types of habits? These habits are what Charles Duhigg refers to as Keystone Habits.

6.4. Keystone Habits

What is a keystone? Google Dictionary tells us that it's "a central stone at the summit of an arch, locking the whole together". This means that a keystone is a sort of foundation, a core asset.

A keystone habit is a habit that serves as a foundation for other habits and as a foundation for positivity.

Keystone habits give you greater mindfulness, less stress, better health, greater willpower, and a myriad of benefits that spill over into other areas of your life by causing a chain reaction.

Keystone Habits encourage change by creating structures that help other habits to thrive and prosper. With these structures in place, they create chain reactions of positive benefits that trickle down and spill over to other habits and areas in your life.

They provide their own set of small wins and a positive feedback loop of benefits that accumulate into lasting change. Combining this with the positive feedback loop of 1-Minute Habits makes the chances of progress and success evermore likely and more pronounced.

Positive keystone habits snowball into changes that are even unrelated to the keystone habit, and these unrelated changes are transformative themselves and cause even more changes, all snowballing, and ultimately culminating in widespread positive changes.

These habits all take willpower to begin with, but they end up giving back far more willpower than they take. Their benefits will spill over into areas like stress reduction, health improvements, increased HRV, as well as many others.

Do you want to know specific habits that can reduce stress, improve health, increase your HRV, AND give you a range of other benefits? Then check out the next 3 sections where I go through 3 universal keystone habits - meditation, exercise, and sleep hygiene.

6.5. Universal Keystone Habits

6.5.1. Meditation

When we use willpower, we are making a conscious decision to do a specific action, an action that usually coincides with our goals. We exert the pause-and-plan response. By pausing-and-planning, we make a conscious effort to resist our impulses and continue towards those goals. So to train and strengthen our willpower, we must pause-and-plan. We must put ourselves in a situation where we are tempted to do one thing but choose to resist and do another. So if we want to lose weight, we could buy loads of sweets and chocolates and put them in front of our faces and then push them away without eating them. We could. But that sounds pretty damn hard. Instead we can use one of the best, direct, and simplest ways to continually induce the pause-and-plan response, continually try to resist urges, and consistently strengthen our willpower, and that is by meditating.

Like the word *sports*, the word *meditation* encompasses a variety of different practices. Meditation usually involves making a conscious effort to self-regulate the mind. This self-regulation is often used to clear the mind, and/or generate a specific emotional state, and/or achieve self-awareness.

Neuroscientists have shown that people who meditate regularly not only become better at meditation, but also other areas of their life - a spillover effect. A meta-analysis of 163 studies was done on meditation and found that it reduces negative emotions, improves attention, focus, impulse control, and mindfulness.[45] Meditation literally reshapes our brains and makes them thicker in some areas[46] - similar to how working out a muscle makes it bigger and stronger. It also increases heart rate variability which is the best physiological measure of our willpower reserve.[47]

Without a doubt, then, meditation strengthens our willpower (as well as a whole load of other great benefits which also in turn strengthen willpower).

Pretty awesome, right? So why don't more people perform this extremely beneficial action? The reason stems from all the misconceptions people have about meditation. The most common of these are: It takes years of practice to be 'good' at it and receive its benefits; it only works if you are good at thinking about nothing; and it's only for religious/spiritual people. All of these points are false. To become 'good' at meditating you don't need to be a spiritual monk and reside in the Himalayas for 50 years. Meditation is simply a pre-frontal cortex workout that trains your mind to focus, pause and plan, and strengthen your willpower. Anyone can do it. To be 'good' and receive its benefits doesn't mean you have to be good at thinking of nothing.

The simplest form of meditation, and the one I did that helped me, is breath meditation. Breath meditation simply involves sitting still and focusing on your breath. By doing it, you can reap all of the benefits of meditation. In the next chapter, I will show you exactly how to do this with 1-Minute Habits.

Let's move onto the 2nd universal keystone habit - exercise.

6.5.2. Exercise

Ah, exercise. Where do I begin listing and explaining all the benefits exercise can bring into your life? Not only does it make you fitter and look trimmer, it induces a *huge* range of other positive changes. Meta-analyses on exercise found that exercise reduces stress, anxiety and depression.[48] It is one of the most under-utilised anti-anxiety and anti-depressant 'drug' there is. Like meditation, exercise gives back far more energy and willpower than it requires and it makes your brain bigger and faster.[49] It increases your heart rate variability.[50] It increases your attention span, makes you less impulsive and makes it easier to resist cravings like binge-eating chocolate.[51]

In *The Power of Habit*, Duhigg wrote, "When people start

habitually exercising, even as infrequently as once a week, they start changing other, unrelated patterns in their lives, often unknowingly. Typically, people who exercise start eating better and becoming more productive at work. They smoke less and show more patience with colleagues and family. They use their credit cards less frequently and say they feel less stressed."

Pretty amazing, right? It induces widespread positive improvements in areas we don't even target. Psychology Professor James Prochaska states that, "Exercise spills over. There's something about it that makes other good habits easier." Exercise strengthens our willpower, improves our health and productivity, reduces stress, reduces impulsiveness and cravings, reduces how much we procrastinate, gives us more control over our emotions and makes us better off all round.

So how much exercise do we need to do to start reaping these glorious benefits? According to a meta-analysis on exercise, we only need to do a couple of minutes of exercise![52] The only 'caveat', if you can even call it that, is you should do it outside, in the presence of nature to get the most benefits in the least amount of time. This 'green exercise' will reduce stress, improve your mood, focus, and self-control. So committing to a short walk around the block or walking your dog can have profound positive effects for you. In general, shorter bouts of exercise have a more powerful and immediate effect on your *brain* (greater mood, stronger willpower, less stress etc.) than longer exhausting bouts.

If you can't go outside for whatever reason, then you can, of course, still reap benefits of exercise indoors (from sit-ups or push-ups, to eager housecleaning and dancing). If the prospect of exercise scares you, don't worry. By adopting a 1-Minute Exercise Habit, you'll be able to ease yourself into it, and still gain its benefits. Whatever your level of fitness, you don't need to sweat profusely and exhaust yourself to get some good exercise. There are hundreds upon hundreds of different ways to exercise and thousands of workouts available for free online, so it has never been easier for us to get started with an exercise habit. And with 1-Minute Habits, it gets even *easier.*

In the next chapter, I will show you how you can apply the 1-Minute Habits System to exercise. For now, let's look at one more exceptional way to strengthen our willpower and make our lives better - via Sleep Hygiene.

6.5.3. Sleep Hygiene

Sleep deprivation increases your stress levels and makes you cranky.[53] I'm sure all of us have had a bad night's sleep at some point and can attest to this. It is harder for you to control your emotions and focus when you are sleep deprived. Meta-analyses on sleep deprivation found that it strongly impairs human functioning and our mood.[54]

I've mentioned how blood glucose is your body's energy source. Well, sleep deprivation makes it harder for your body to absorb glucose, hence you feel more tired and exhausted, and more tempted by sugar and caffeine. It makes your pre-frontal cortex tired and become mildly dysfunctional.[55] This state it's in is similar to a mildly drunk person.[56] In this impaired state, our basal ganglia has to help us out and go into auto-pilot more often. Our pre-frontal cortex not being able to work properly and absorb energy sufficiently makes us have less control over ourselves. We become more impulsive and prone to give in to cravings, more stressed and irritable, and we have lower willpower. Sucks, right? The good news is that all this is reversible from getting a good night's sleep.[57] Once you are well-rested, the mild dysfunction will go away, and your mood and willpower should go back to their regular state.

So to avoid and/or reverse all these negativities, make sure you get a good night's sleep! And if you find yourself lacking in willpower, one thing you can do is look at how much sleep you are getting and change it for the better. This is easier said than done for some people though.

A bit more about my experience with sleep deprivation

I was in a negative loop of sleep deprivation: I'd constantly feel tired and stressed all day from the lack of sleep; then I'd act impulsive and binge-eat and procrastinate; then I'd stay up late because my mind wasn't tired, and was too stressed because of the unproductive decisions I made in the day; then I couldn't sleep for more than 4 hours, sometimes even less; then I'd start my day; and repeat.

Doctors couldn't really help, and any advice I'd get from anyone would just be too overwhelming for me to follow. It was too daunting for someone whose brain was in a 'mildly drunk' state. And if I did try to apply that advice, I would burn myself out and give up.

With 1-Minute Habits, I was able to get out of the negative loop I was in, and reap the benefits of improved sleep hygiene (as well as the benefits of Meditation and Exercise). My sleep hygiene isn't perfect yet, but the improvements so far have given me a better mood, and more energy, than I've had in a long time. These benefits then spilled over into other areas, like giving me more energy to exercise, which then in turn gave me even more benefits. 1-Minute Habits put me in a positive loop.

***

Sleep hygiene is different from other 1-Minute Habits in this book as it can encompass a few other habits (like meditation and exercise) into it. For more detail, see the next chapter.

6.6. Personal Keystone Habits

We have the above 3 universal keystone habits, but they aren't the only ones. They are universal due to their clear evidence of benefits and their popularity. They will bring about their benefits for anyone. However, we all have our own individualities and circumstances, so there may be some personal habits that can fit into our lives specifically, and give us the benefits of a keystone habit. These personal keystone habits will provide us with chain reactions of benefits and lead to improvements in more than 1 area of our lives.

To find personal keystone habits, you will have to ask yourself what changes and actions you can do on a consistent basis that you think will have profound effects for you personally. Don't worry if you can't think of any. This is just to show you that great improvements aren't only enabled by adopting the universal keystone habits. However, the universal keystone habits are, without a doubt, one of the best places for you to start if you are not sure what to do. On your 1-Minute Habit journey, I strongly recommend you adopt at least one of those habits, so that you can reap their benefits which will make it easier to form other habits.

6.7. Chapter 6 Key Facts

- Willpower is like a muscle. It can be drained, and it can be trained.
- 1-Minute Habits, uncomfortable actions, reducing stress, improving health, and increasing heart rate variance, all train and strengthen willpower.
- Keystone Habits strengthen willpower in a vast amount of ways, as well as providing a chain reaction of other benefits.

Chapter 7: 1-Minute Habit Examples

Success is the sum of small efforts - repeated day in and day
out.
- Robert Collier

Practice yourself, for heaven's sake in little things, and then
proceed to greater.
- Epictetus

Consistency trumps intensity; all the time. That intensity is
born from consistency.
- Mark Reifkind

7.1. The examples are not exhaustive

Here, I will show you how to apply the 4 steps of the 1-Minute Habits System to a number of popular and beneficial habits. There are 9 in total, and I'll start with the universal keystone habits. You can skim through this chapter, or read specific habits only, or read it all intently. You can also skip it entirely for now and head on to the Final Words section at the end of the book. This chapter is to just show you exactly how the 4 steps can be applied to a vast range of popular habits.

You should NOT try to form all of these 1-Minute Habits at once. You also don't have to strictly follow the specifics of the examples either. Everyone's situation will be different so they may define, set-up cues, and do the same type of 1-Minute Habit differently. Therefore the examples will be conventional. In each example I've given further explanations in square brackets. All in all, this chapter will give you a broader sense of how the 1-Minute Habits System can be applied to just about anything.

7.2. 1-Minute Universal Keystone Habits

7.2.1. Meditation

I will explain to you the simplest form of meditation - breath meditation - and show how you can reap its benefits for you.

Breath Meditation simply involves sitting still and focusing on your breath. You have to focus on breathing deeply and slowly (which helps to increase HRV[58]).

Whilst meditating, you will have a lot of other thoughts, urges, and distractions that prevent you from focusing on your breath. When this happens, people tend to assume they can't and shouldn't meditate because it won't work for them. That's where they are wrong.

Once thoughts start flying in, all you have to do is eventually notice them and bring your focus back onto breathing slowly. You may notice your thoughts drift away quickly, or it may take you a while to notice this.

However long you take, as long as you bring your thoughts back to your breath, you will be doing what meditation is for. You will be pausing-and-planning, and be mindful. This specific act of clearing your mind over and over is *how* you benefit from meditating. And this is how your willpower strengthens as you are exerting self-control. In being conscious of your mind wanting to take the easy way out (get lost in thoughts), and then controlling it to do what's right (focusing on breath), you are being self-aware and then self-regulating.

Psychologist Kelly McGonigal wrote in her book, *The*

Willpower Instinct, that "Meditation is not about getting rid of all your thoughts; it's learning not to get so lost in them that you forget what your goal [goal in this case is focusing on breath] is." So being bad at meditating is actually the point. The worse you are at it then the more pronounced its benefits will be for you.

From meditating, we will teach our minds how to handle inner and outer distractions. If we feel extremely distracted, frustrated and fidgety whilst meditating we assume that we're wasting our time. But studies show that, even if our meditation is filled with lots of distractions, our focus *outside* of meditation should increase.[59]

Here's a typical example that someone might create when applying the 1-Minute Habits System to meditation.

Example

1) Define - Visualise and Simplify

Visualise: [*Answer the following questions: What are your goals? What do you want to achieve? What accomplishment will give you the most fulfilment?*]

My goal is to be less stressed, so I can be healthier and happier. I have made a mental picture of that, and I know it will give me fulfilment.

[*Other Goals: Strengthen willpower; greatly improve many areas of my life; have more control over thoughts and actions etc.*]

Simplify:

Round 1: A core repetitive action (habit) that can help me reduce stress is breath meditation.

Round 2: A scaled-down, easy version of meditation that I can do every day with ease is 1-Minute Breath Meditation. [*Another example: Focus on taking 5 deep, slow breaths.*]

My Defined 1-Minute Habit to reduce stress is 1-Minute Breath Meditation.

2) Cue set-up

When cue: [*Decide when in the day you want to do your 1-Minute Habit.*]

I will do my 1-Minute Breath Meditation whenever I am free during the day, so I have an open approach for my when-cue.

I don't really need to add positive or negative cues because of how easy this action will be.

[*Examples of positive cues you could use for 1-Minute Meditation: Reduce the noise levels to make it easier and more relaxed to meditate by closing your room's windows, door, and/or putting in ear plugs, and creating a seating arrangement beforehand such as a comfortable seat, or space on the floor, or a meditation mat.*]

3) Chains Tracking

I printed a yearly calendar, labelled it 1-Minute Meditation, put it up on my wall, and then I also downloaded a chains tracking app on my phone and created a 1-Minute Meditation chain on it.

4) 1-Minute Meditation

I will do my 1-Minute Breath Meditation every day and over-perform whenever I want to, but only plan to do 1-Minute.

The actions involved: Set a 1-Minute timer. Sit still. Eyes closed. Take deep breaths. Focus on breath. Focus on inhaling and exhaling. Bring thoughts back to breath as much as I can.

Stop once timer goes off, or decide to over-perform after 1-Minute, and set a longer timer.

[A bit more detail on doing this 1-Minute Habit. It is good to practise, whilst meditating, making each whole breath last around 10 seconds. Then maintain your breaths at this length, or make them last even longer. Aim to slow your breath to 4-6 breaths per minute. This won't happen straight away, it'll happen over time, so work on making your breath deep and slowing it down. This activates the pre-frontal cortex and increases HRV.

So focus on inhaling for 5 seconds and exhaling for 5 seconds. And don't hold your breath (that builds stress). Inhale deeply - feel your stomach and chest expand. Then exhale very slowly and gently. Prolong your exhale, then inhale deeply once you can't exhale anymore and repeat.

The hardest part, of course, is the impatience and urge to stop, and difficulty in keeping thoughts at bay. But realise that this is normal and part of the process. Simply work gradually towards being conscious of your thoughts, then feel the urges, impulses and resistance and breathe them away, and go back to focusing on your inhaling and exhaling.

Besides, this is the important part. This is the part that is training your self-control. You will find yourself feeling one or more of these: restless, distracted, impatient, and bored. But if you learn to say no to these resistances and go back to focusing on your breath, you will be learning a vital skill that can be applied to all areas of your life.

When feeling the resistance, simply remind yourself that this is normal, and distracted meditation is still beneficial, and that, if you can get through these distractions now, it will be easier to get through them tomorrow. Learning to say no to that voice will teach you how to persevere, so meditation is a great opportunity to learn that valuable skill.

When your meditation skill level increases, you could also then have a temporary 1-Minute Research Habit, to find new and more advanced ways to meditate, then turn that into a 1-Minute Meditation Habit to take your skill even further.]

7.2.2. Exercise

I don't need to mention all the benefits of exercise again. We all know that there are exceptional benefits from doing it. Exercise is a broad term, but whatever the type of exercise you want to do, you can apply the 1-Minute Habits System to it, for optimal efficiency.

Example

1) Define - Visualise and Simplify

Visualise: My goal is to be fitter and healthier as this will make me more confident and happier. A mental picture of me having achieved that goal makes me feel like I will be fulfilled in looking, feeling, and being better. [*Other Goals: Increasing performance in a sport; relieve stress; be more attractive; greatly improve many areas of my life; etc.*]

Simplify:

Round 1: A core repetitive action (habit) that can help me become fitter and healthier is exercise. The exercise that interests me currently is running. [*Pick whatever you want. Other examples: Working out at the gym; working out at home; playing sports; dancing.*]

Round 2: A scaled-down, easy version of running that I can do every day with ease is 1-Minute Walking Outside [*or 1-minute Running Outside*]. [*Other examples: 1-Minute at the gym or drive for 1-Minute to the gym; 1-Minute of push-ups or sit-ups at home/ 5 push-ups or 5 sit-ups at home; kick a ball outside for 1-Minute; or even 1-Minute putting on exercise clothes - this actually works.*]

My Defined 1-Minute Habit to become fitter and healthier is 1-Minute Walking Outside.

2) Cue set-up

When cue: I will do my 1-Minute Walking Outside in the morning. Or whenever I am free. So I have a mixture of a routine and open approach for my when-cue.

A **Positive cue** I will use is to put out my exercise clothes the night before I want to walk, so that I can get ready quicker [*and hence facilitate the 1-Minute Habit*].

[*Other examples of positive cues you could use for 1-Minute Walking Outside: Have an iPod with a kick-ass playlist, and headphones out ready for you to listen to when you walk, and hopefully run when you over-perform; setting out clothing that can handle bad weather, just in case it rains.*]

3) Chains Tracking

I printed a yearly calendar, labelled it 1-Minute Walking Outside, put it up on my wall, and then I also downloaded a chains tracking app on my phone and created a chain for it.

4) 1-Minute Walking Outside

I will do my 1-Minute Walking Outside every day and over-perform whenever I want to, but only plan to ever do 1-Minute.

My over-performing can involve walking for longer, jogging, or running.

[Exercise can be a progressive habit, as it can have a lot of stages, depending on the type of exercise. For example, if you have a low level of fitness like I did, you'd want to start working out at home, and have something like a 1-Minute Home workout, 1-Minute Sit-ups or 1-Minute Push-ups Habit (or a temporary 1-Minute Research Exercise Habit to find a good exercise for you).

Over time, your fitness and confidence will grow, so you may want to move onto a gym. Then you can change your 1-Minute Home workout to 1-Minute Gym workout (or create a new chain entirely).

Then as more time goes on, your skill level will grow even more, and you'll want to work on building your 1-Minute Gym Habit. So you could again have a temporary 1-Minute Workout Research, to figure out the best workout plans, for you, and then turn them into a 1-Minute Habit.

Regardless of your fitness level, whether it's low, or high (but when it is high you would've likely already formed a workout habit), you can implement a 1-Minute Exercise Habit and benefit.]

7.2.3. Sleep Hygiene

Sleep hygiene is different to other 1-Minute Habits because it includes a few 1-Minute Habits and practices within it. Sleep is an integral part of our health and willpower, so it makes sense that we should try to get optimal sleep. I will show you 1-Minute Habits and actions you can do that are conducive to getting effective sleep.

This example will be divided into 4 parts: 1st part) Reducing stress to fall asleep; 2nd part) Associate your bed and the night with sleep; 3rd part) Getting into bed; 4th part) Waking up to your alarm.

Reducing stress to fall asleep

I had a lot of stress and anxiety problems along with a distorted body clock which made it difficult to fall asleep. By working on habits that alleviated stress and made me feel positive in more ways than one, I was able to improve my sleep. So one way to improve your sleep hygiene is to form stress relieving habits. There's no better habits to form to help with sleep than meditation and exercise, since they are keystone habits as well. Other stress relieving habits include reading, to help you wind down before bed, or being more positive, to diminish the stress of your problems.

Associate your bed and the night with sleep

Associate your bed mainly with sleep. So don't eat, watch TV, sit with your laptop, or read books in bed. This will condition your mind to know when it's time to sleep (as soon as you get into bed).

When the sun goes down, dim the lights in your house, and lower the brightness of your computers and phones if you find yourself staring at them at night for long periods. Your mind will condition itself that low light is a sign to wind down, relax, and sleep. This is what we do naturally anyway when it's night, but with the immense light sources we put in front of our faces these days, we can distort this natural instinct.

We should also do the opposite to help with sleep association. Be exposed to light during the day-time. So open up your curtains during the day, and get yourself out in the sun.

Getting into bed

A problem with our sleep might not be that we find it difficult to fall asleep, but that we find it difficult to get into bed. There might be some distractions that for some reason seem extra appealing at night. Such as, watching late night TV, or just texting on our phones. What we need to do in this case is find what is distracting us from getting into bed at a routine time. We must make it harder to do those things, and make it easier to get into bed. So we can set-up negative cues and positive cues.

Negative cues depend on your personal distractions. If it is TV that's distracting you, get your energised self, say after dinner, to make it harder for your future night-time self to watch TV. So take out the plugs, or put away the TV remote. Whatever your distraction is, increase the decision-making process in doing it. If it's the Internet that's distracting you, download software that can block websites at a specific time like the StayFocusd Google Chrome extension or SelfControl app for Macs. You can also download software that shuts your computer off automatically at a specific time like Switch Off. Technology may hamper your sleep but it can also help you. Try searching online for other more pertinent software for yourself.

If cues don't help, then you can also try replacing your night-time bad habits with good habits like reading. Reading can be a good replacement for entertainment and distraction. It can help you wind down, and not expose you to bright light like TVs, computers, and phones do.

Another reason you may be so put off by getting into bed at a normal time might be because your night-time routine is too tedious for your tired night time self. For this, you could implement positive cues to make it easier to do things like brushing your teeth, washing your face, wiping off your makeup, changing clothes, etc. Instead of waiting to do your night time routine when you are tired, do it earlier. So set out your change of clothes beforehand, and brush your teeth earlier, like straight after dinner.

You could even set an alarm on your phone to remind you to do this.

Waking up to your alarm

Sometimes, even if we get into bed at an optimal time and get a good night's sleep, getting out of bed when our alarm goes off can still be quite hard. If we are so used to hitting the snooze button, then it gets even harder. What we can do here is have a *1-Minute Alarm Conditioning Habit.*

By getting ourselves out of bed early, we are likelier to get into bed early too. And by getting out of bed early in the morning, we'll help to fix our body clock, if it is distorted. So this 1-Minute Habit can positively affect most parts of getting good sleep hygiene, and so can help you fall asleep. For this reason, I will apply the 1-Minute Habits System's 4 steps to 1-Minute Alarm Conditioning.

So what does 1-Minute Alarm Conditioning entail?

The best way to get our minds used to getting out of bed when our alarms go off is to literally practice doing just that. Simply go to your bed at whatever time you want, set an alarm to go off in the next minute, and then get into bed. While in bed, close your eyes and visualise getting out of bed, affirm to yourself that you will get out of bed, and remind yourself of the reasons why you should (e.g. you set that alarm for a reason; what can you accomplish whilst in bed?).

Once your alarm goes off, open your eyes, jump out of bed, turn your alarm off, and walk out your room, promptly, without much conscious effort at all. Just go through the motions and don't think about them. You can practice this conditioning however many times you want. And for good measure, make your alarm something specific, that you only use for waking up.

What you will be doing is conditioning your mind to act exactly how you want it to in the morning when the alarm goes off. Over time, you will reshape your mind and do these actions in the morning.

Example

1) Define - Visualise and Simplify

Visualise: I want to get up earlier in the day so that I can get more work done. I also want to improve my sleep and feel more energetic and healthier. This all can be done by conditioning myself to wake up early as soon as my alarm goes off. Imagining having more energy, and more time in the day to do work is something that can help me reach fulfilment as I'll have more time to work on the things that matter.

Simplify:

Round 1: The habit I want to form is waking up when my alarm goes off.

Round 2: I can do this easily via 1-Minute Alarm Conditioning.

2) Cue set-up

When-cue: I will do this whenever I am free so I'll have an open approach.

Positive cues: I will put my alarm far away from my bed to further urge myself to get out. [*You could also put your alarm outside your room, or even in the bathroom to get yourself out there to start your day. Other positive cues: have a glass or bottle of water that you can chug as soon as you get out of bed to associate the reward of fulfilling your thirst with the act of getting out of bed.*]

3) Chains Tracking

I have printed a calendar and created a chain via a Chains Tracking App, and labelled it 1-Minute Alarm Conditioning.

4) 1-Minute Alarm Conditioning

I will do this whenever I can during the day. Over-performing will involve me doing this 1-Minute Habit more than once.

7.3. Other Popular Habits

7.3.1. Reading

Most of the personal problems we face have been experienced by someone else and written about in a book.

It was reading books and research that gave me the knowledge on how to sort my life out.

It was reading that gave you the valuable knowledge of this book.

There are so many reasons why we should read, for instance: reading can be pleasurable; help you relax and reduce stress; improve your focus and concentration; improve your memory; stimulate your mind and imagination; make you smarter; make you more interesting.

So whether it be for learning, pleasure, or both, reading is extremely valuable.

Example

1) Define - Visualise and Simplify

Visualise: My goal is to read more books so I can expand my mind [*or any of the benefits mentioned*]. From visualising and getting a mental picture of achieving this goal, I feel like I'll be smarter, sharper, and more imaginative. This will give me a sense of fulfilment.

Simplify:

Round 1: The repeated action (habit) will be to simply read books.

Round 2: So reading simplified will be 1-Minute Reading [*or read 1 page or 1 paragraph*].

2) Cue set-up

When cue: I'd like to read whenever I am free and feel like learning or winding down. So I will have an open approach.

[*Positive cues examples: Buy books you find interesting beforehand, so you will always have something you want to read; have a quiet location (e.g. certain room) that you want to use for reading*]

3) Chains Tracking

I have printed a calendar and downloaded a chains app. I labelled my calendar, and created a chain for 1-Minute Reading.

4) 1-Minute Reading

I will plan to read for a minute every day, and stop if I feel like it, or over-perform by reading more.

7.3.2. Writing

Example

1) Define - Visualise and Simplify

Visualise: My goal is to write more books so I can express myself better and teach others [*Other goals: finish an assignment; finish a dissertation; write a book; create a blog with consistent content; etc.*]. From visualising and getting a mental picture of achieving this goal, I feel like it would truly bring me value and fulfilment.

Simplify:

Round 1: The repeated action (habit) will be to simply write something.

Round 2: So writing simplified will be 1-Minute Writing [*or write 1 paragraph; write 1 page; 1-Minute researching how to write, through books or online research*].

2) Cue set-up

When cue: I'd like to write whenever I'm free and feel like putting whatever is on my mind on paper. So I will have an open approach.

[*Positive cues examples: Have writing equipment out, organised, and ready to use (e.g. notepad and pen, and/ or laptop); have a quiet location (e.g.*

certain room) that you want to use for writing.]

3) Chains Tracking.

I have printed a calendar and downloaded a chains app. I labelled my calendar, and created a chain for 1-Minute Writing.

4) 1-Minute Writing

I will plan to write for a minute every day, and stop if I feel like it, or over-perform by writing more.

[*Writing can also be progressive. Example stages: 1st stage - write at your current skill level (don't worry about it being good); 2nd stage - research how to write and apply the knowledge; 3rd stage - get your writing out there and share it to get feedback (show it to family, friends, online forums, create a blog etc.); 4th stage - write a book.*

You can also have a temporary 1-Minute Writing Research Habit to learn and figure out what to write, and/or how to write better. But this can come later. It's good to first start out with just writing whatever you can and ingraining that habit into yourself first.]

7.3.3. Learning/Studying

Start studying as soon as your semester begins. I know it's so damn tempting to put it off. And that's what I did when I was at school and university. But I would've saved myself from so, so, so much stress and guilt if I had just started doing a tiny amount every day, instead of starting and panicking a few weeks or days before deadlines. Save yourself the stress and guilt by doing a tiny bit every day. You'll also be able to enjoy things more without having the stress of needing to study rampant in your head.

Of course, studying is not confined to schools and universities. The real studying and learning begins after your academic education is done, in my opinion.

So let's apply the 1-Minute Habits System.

Example

1) Define - Visualise and Simplify

Visualise: I want to learn more about a subject that I am interested in, in the hope that I can apply it and enhance my skills. The mental picture I see from learning this skill makes me feel happy and fulfilled, as this skill is something that really interests me [*other goal examples: I want to study for an exam or assignment; I want to increase my employability prospects; I want to learn for the sake of learning; I want to improve myself and my knowledge*].

Simplify:

Round 1: I want to form a habit of learning about that subject [*you could also tie in a reading or writing 1-Minute Habit into this*].

Round 2: I will spend a minute learning about the subject I'm interested in. This learning can include reading, researching, writing, practising, watching relevant videos - basically anything that improves my knowledge and skill of it.

This will be my 1-Minute Learning [*insert subject/ skill*] Habit.

2) Cue set-up

When-cue: I will study after work on weekdays, and whenever I am free on weekends. So a mix of a routine and open approach.

Positive cues: I will create a clear tidy workspace for studying, and have all my studying tools ready.

Negative cues: I procrastinate a lot on certain websites when on the Internet, so I will temporarily block them whilst learning.

3) Chains Tracking

I have printed a calendar and downloaded a chains app. I labelled my calendar and created a chain for 1-Minute [*insert subject/skill*] Learning.

4) 1-Minute Learning

I will plan to learn more about my specific topic of interest every day for at least a minute, and over-perform when in motion.

[*Learning will, of course, have many stages - the number of which depends upon what subject or skill you are learning about. It is useful to focus on assimilating the basics and fundamentals, and once they are internalised, you can move onto more advanced topics of your subject. You could even create a temporary 1-Minute Habit to research about the most effective learning techniques. And you could also create a temporary 1-Minute Learning Habit for when you have deadlines approaching if you are in academic education. Lots of variation and flexibility.*

When it comes to learning anything new, it will seem difficult at first. Just keep going at it, even when you don't get it. Not understanding and finding it difficult is normal and part of the process. As time goes by and you have remained consistent, eventually what you've learnt will all assimilate and click together to build and broaden your understanding. A bit like magic. So you may not be able to connect the dots moving forward. But when you look back you'll see that they've connected. Trust that they'll connect and keep persistent.]

7.3.4. Cleaning

According to the study 'No place like home'[60], the mess and clutter in our homes can be a major source of stress - so the tidier our homes, the happier we may be. Therefore, de-cluttering and cleaning our homes is a great way to alleviate stress and feel better. This, in a sense, will then also de-clutter our minds.

As well as making our surroundings look nicer, and alleviating stress, cleaning also involves physical activity, so it can benefit us in more ways than one. We all have probably felt at one point that we have too much cleaning to do and would rather put it off because of how overwhelming it seems. So what better way to overcome this problem and gain all the benefits of cleaning than by adopting a 1-Minute Cleaning Habit?

Like 1-Minute Learning/Studying, 1-Minute Cleaning is also a broad term, and therefore can encompass a number of little actions.

Example

1) Define - Visualise and Simplify

Visualise: My goal is to clean my home so that it doesn't build up and require more effort later. I feel that cleaning my home will help to prevent the stress of an unorganised and messy home, which will make me feel better.

Simplify:

Round 1: The habit will be to clean something.

Round 2: A habit initiator of cleaning will be 1-Minute Cleaning. 1-Minute Cleaning can encompass any sort of cleaning so 1-Minute: Vacuuming or Vacuum 1 room; Decluttering; Sweeping; Scrubbing; Surface Wiping, or Wipe 1 Surface; Washing 1 Dish; etc.

Each simple action will likely urge me into doing more cleaning overall. And by being consistent with cleaning, even a tiny amount, it will help prevent mess from getting out of hand.

2) Cue set-up

When cue: Anytime I am free, and/or anytime a mess is bothering me. So there is a mix of both approaches (open and routine).

[*Positive cues examples: Have a stock of cleaning supplies available and make them easily accessible; if cleaning seems too tedious, set out an mp3 player and headphones, with music or audiobooks - this can facilitate the act of cleaning by making it less boring.*]

3) Chains Tracking

I have printed a calendar and downloaded a chains app. I labelled my calendar and created a chain for 1-Minute Cleaning.

4) 1-Minute Cleaning

I will plan to clean my home for a minute every day, and stop if I feel like it, or over-perform by cleaning more.

7.3.5. Public Speaking

A relevant quote from Jerry Seinfeld in an episode of *Seinfeld*: "According to most studies, people's number one fear is public speaking. Number two is death. Death is number two. Does that sound right? This means to the average person, if you go to a funeral, you're better off in the casket than doing the eulogy."

Now most of those studies are kind of questionable. And I'm sure we'd all agree that that we'd all prefer public speaking to death. But with society safer today than it's ever been, the fear of death isn't something we think about all that often. Public speaking, though, is a more relevant fear. But why is it so terrifying?

In the book *The Real Story of Risk* by Glenn Croston, he states that our fear of public speaking stems from our primitive ancestors' fear of predators. Over the last few million years, as humans evolved, we were in a world filled with large predators out to get us. Those who had the highest chance of survival were those who were in groups. There is power in numbers. Ostracism then (rejected or banished from a group), would mean that you'd have to fight for survival on your own.

A big fear in public speaking comes from being embarrassed or judged and being ostracised (socially rejected). Primitively speaking, social rejection would ultimately lead to death. So the brain's seemingly irrational fear of public speaking may be due to its survival instincts from back in the day.

It's unfortunate, and what's worse is that this fear of social rejection isn't confined to public speaking. It is faced by anyone who has to face a crowd or group of people, or even a single person.

But as with anything, the more experience we have with it, then the more comfortable it will feel. For any fear or discomfort, we can apply 1-Minute Habits to ease ourselves into it, incrementally.

Example

1) Define - Visualise and Simplify

Visualise: My goal is to be more confident [*other examples of goals: give engaging presentations and lectures; improve my charisma; become better at socialising; etc.*].

Simplify:

Round 1: A habit I want to form to reach this goal is to practice my public speaking repetitively, starting off with simply practicing in front of a mirror.

Round 2: By simplifying the habit to get a super easy action I can do every day, I created 1-Minute Public Speaking Practice [*or 1-Minute Mirror Speaking*].

2) Cue set-up

When-cue: Do this every day before I go out, or whenever I am free and near a mirror. I have a mix of a routine and open approach.

Positive cues: I will sometimes decide on a topic to speak about beforehand that I want to practice with. And, depending on the importance of the topic, I may make some notes to memorise, and practice speaking them. I will then leave these notes in a prominent location to remind me, and to facilitate my 1-Minute Habit.

3) Chains Tracking

I printed a calendar and downloaded a chains app, and labelled them accordingly.

4) 1-Minute Public Speaking Practice

I will speak in front of a mirror every day for 1-Minute. I will over-perform if I feel like it whilst doing the 1-Minute Habit.

[*Public Speaking is, of course, a progressive habit. You can start with speaking in front of a mirror for weeks or months until you have it internalised and are ready to practice it in other areas. Some example stages to move up to with public speaking are: 1st stage - 1-Minute of practice speaking in front of a mirror; 2nd stage - 1-Minute practice speaking in front of someone you are close to like a parent, sibling, or best-friend; 3rd stage - 1-Minute practice speaking in front of a group of friends; 4th stage - 1-Minute practice speaking in front of a camera and uploading that online in places that are relevant, welcoming, and can give you feedback; 5th stage - join a public speaking class; 6th stage - 1-Minute practice in front of a big crowd - incrementally increasing the size of the crowd as your comfort increases.*

Of course, these stages are simply examples, and you don't have to follow them. You may come up with your own examples and stages, and order of stage progression that are better. Please don't feel confined by the examples of this chapter. You can follow them, or use them as a guideline to come up with a better and more relevant example.

Also, you could add a temporary habit, or even make it a stage to progress to, where you research and learn about how to become better at public speaking.]

7.3.6. Positivity

Always keep your smile. That's how I explain my long life.
- Jeanne Calment.

The more you worry, the better you get at it, and then the more you'll worry. The more your thoughts are positive then the more your thoughts become positive. Repetition in the way we think and do things will determine who we'll become.

By just working on having one conscious positive thought a day, you can start shifting the momentum of your mindset into becoming happier. And by becoming positive, your problems, and negative affects in general, will have less of a hold on you which will leave you with more time and energy to do the things that matter.

I mentioned in chapter 3 that rest and food can replenish our willpower. Another thing to add to that list are *Positive Affects*[61]. If you feel good, you do good. So having a consistent 1-Minute Habit where you induce a positive affect on yourself daily, could have great benefits for you in the long-run.

Example

1) Define - Visualise and Simplify

Visualise: My goal is to be more positive. Being more positive will help me to have better control over my problems, and will help me to spread joy [*other goals: perceive my misfortunes as opportunities; be happier; be kinder; feel fulfilled; etc.*]

Simplify:

Round 1: The habit of positivity can involve thinking positive thoughts.
Round 2: So spending at least 1-Minute a day thinking

positively, such as reflecting over and thinking about the positive actions I did during the day or about the general positivity in my life.

So my defined 1-Minute Habit will be a 1-Minute Positive Thinking Habit.

[Other examples: in the study 'Grin and Bear it[62]', they found that forcing yourself to smile can reduce stress and induce a positive affect, so you could have a 1-Minute Smiling Habit; if you want an even stronger benefit, then forcing yourself to laugh works too. There are many studies[63] that show forcing yourself to laugh can boost your mood, ease pain, and help fight infections. What you'd find very relevant is that a study[64] even found that forced laughing for exactly a minute can boost your mood, and make you more positive. With that said, then, a 1-Minute Laughing Habit is an extremely powerful method to boost your mood and/ or condition yourself to be more positive.]

2) Cue set-up

When cue: I'd like to think positively whenever I am free and alone in a quiet place. So I'll have an open approach.

[Positive cues: you could write or print a motivating and positive quote that you like and put it up in a prominent location - so every time you see it you'll feel more positive. And once the positive effects of that quote have diminished, take it off and put up a different positive quote.

You can also do this with passwords. Find yourself constantly logging into a specific website? Change the password to something motivational and positive (AND SECURE!), to inject positivity into your day. Then once this password loses its effect, change it.

You could even use variations of both these positive cues for other 1-Minute Habits.]

3) Chains Tracking

I have printed a calendar and downloaded a chains app. I labelled my calendar, and created a chain for 1-Minute Positive Thinking.

4) 1-Minute Positive Thinking

I will plan to think positively for a minute every day, then stop if I feel like it, or over-perform by thinking and reflecting some more.

7.4. Apply 1-Minute Habits everywhere and in different ways

It doesn't end there. There are, of course, many other 1-Minute Habits to form outside of these examples. 1-Minute Habits can be applied to just about every single positive habit you want to adopt. If you want to be better at something, you can apply 1-Minute Habits to it. If there's anything that you want to do, apply 1-Minute Habits.

A reminder: I've gone through 9 examples of 1-Minute Habits. That's a lot of 1-Minute Habits. And in no way should you try to form all of them at once. There may be a lot of new habits you want to form, and there's a lot I'd like to form as well, but trying to change too much too quickly is inefficient.

A study even shows that we overestimate our willpower.[65] Even if you think it won't be a big deal to adopt loads, remember that the effects of ego-depletion can be subtle so you may not even notice your weakened willpower until it is too late. Stick with 1-4 (especially in the beginning), with at *least* 1 being a keystone habit.

Different ways to apply 1-Minute Habits:

1-Minute Habits can be done more than once a day

As with over-performing, which you can do as much or as little as possible, 1-Minute Habits can be done however many times you want during the day. If you have a habit like studying for exams or cleaning the house, you can initiate your 1-Minute Habit to start, do it, over-perform or not, and then increase your chain (for the day). Then, later on in the day, you can initiate your 1-Minute Habit again to start and do some more work (but you won't do anything with your chain since you already increased it by fulfilling your quota earlier).

Temporary 1-Minute Habits for deadlines

If circumstances permit, you can adopt a temporary 1-Minute Habit to supplement other 1-Minute Habits for a goal.

You can also create stand-alone temporary 1-Minute Habits for when you have, say, a deadline approaching. If you have a project to finish at a set time but you're feeling overwhelmed, distracted, demotivated, and procrastinating, you can apply 1-Minute Habits. You can eliminate all these feelings of resistance in starting by scaling down your task and turning it into a 1-Minute Habit. Then, once you have started, you can over-perform as much as you can.

And then, later on in the day, you can initiate this 1-Minute Habit again. Once you've reached your deadline you can let go of this 1-Minute Habit. So 1-Minute Habits don't have to be confined only to long-term goal achieving and habit forming. They can be applied in many ways.

1-off 1-Minute Habits

Another way is that you can form an even more temporary version of 1-Minute Habits for whenever you have to do a 1-off task. So for example, if you have visitors coming over and your house is a mess, you can initiate a 1-Minute Habit for 1 day only that eliminates resistance and gets you to start cleaning.

***

Apply 1-Minute Habits for your long-term goals to achieve what you want. Apply them for temporary actions. You can apply them in just about any area of your life.

Remember this: **If you ever feel resistance when you want to do something, turn it into a 1-Minute Habit**. Are you putting something off that you know you should be doing? Turn it into a 1-Minute Habit. Get creative and find other ways to make 1-Minute Habits work for you.

7.5. Chapter 7 Key Facts

- Form any habit with 1-Minute Habits.
- Form 1-Minute Keystone Habits and reap tremendous benefits.

Final Words

Action is the foundational key to all success.
- Pablo Picasso

Your past is not your potential. In any hour you can choose to
liberate the future.
- Marilyn Ferguson

1-Minute Habits liberate you

Phew. So we've come a long way, but we've made it.

Science has shown us how our old ways are ineffective. We have learnt that 1-Minute Habits revolve around our brain's design and are conducive to success. They also provide a self-boosting feedback loop that will make us feel good instead of constantly like a failure. 1-Minute Habits take into account the most important determinants of success and fulfilment - consistency and willpower. With 1-Minute Habits you will be consistent, and you will optimise your brain and its willpower.

You know how to apply the system in 4 simple and easy steps:

1) Define - Visualise your goal(s) to see what to prioritise, and simplify it into a habit. Then simplify the habit into a 1-Minute Habit.
2) Cue set-up - Decide when you will do your 1-Minute Habit during the day.
3) Chains Tracking - Print/Draw/Buy a calendar, label it, and start updating it once you reach your 1-Minute Habit quota. Download a relevant app to track on the go.
4) 1-Minute Habit - Do your 1-Minute Habit and then over-perform as much or as little as you want, or not at all.

You also know how to strengthen your willpower, and how to apply it to these 4 steps.

The core message of *1-Minute Habits* is to liberate you. We are not always in a peak performance state, and yet our old strategies expect us to be. 1-Minute Habits give you an incremental approach that takes into account our fluctuating performance levels so that you can improve regardless of how you feel. That in itself is liberating. But you will also be liberated from the downward spiral of our old ways; and, more importantly, liberated from the false notion that you are weak.

This brings me to the end of the book. Thank you so much for taking the time to read it. I hope this book helps you to start a journey filled with consistent small wins that accumulate into long-lasting fulfilment. And I am confident that it will. I have started my 1-Minute Habits journey for a few months now and its benefits for me have been amazing. This is just the beginning and I look forward to seeing how much more I can improve with this system. And I know you'll feel the same way for yourself, when you start.

Of course, until you actually start and do them, you may still have a bit of scepticism. It was only by *doing* that I was truly convinced. And only by *doing* will you be. And it is only by *doing* the things that matter to us, consistently, that we'll get to where we want to be.

So, time to start.

Sincerely,
Raghib Ahmed

Can you do me a favour?

Amazon Review

If you enjoyed *1-Minute Habits*, would you mind taking a minute to write a review on Amazon? Reviewers are such a valuable part of Amazon, and it's so quick and easy to become one. Simply write what you thought of it.[66] Any type of review will help, and will mean so much to me.

Spread the word

And if you have found value in this book, then please do share it with others. If you know anyone who can benefit from this book, let them know about it. Be the first out of your friends and family to share it and start a chain reaction of positivity.

Join the Community!

Facebook

Come and join the 1-Minute Habits community on Facebook.[67] Goals thrive in communities filled with like-minded people so don't miss out. I will also be posting updates on anything 1-Minute Habits related, as well as interesting quotes and reminders on optimising life in general.

Blog

And speaking of optimising life, if you would like to receive free bonus materials, my personal reflections and insights, and exclusive content, then check out my blog and join its email list at raghibahmed.com.[68] I post valuable information weekly, and will post updates on any future projects I'll be working on.

Twitter

You can also stay updated on everything 1-Minute Habits and optimisation related by following me on Twitter @oneminutehabits.[69]

Pinterest

If you prefer a more visual outlet to stay updated, then follow me on Pinterest at www.pinterest.com/oneminutehabits.[70]

YouTube

And finally, check out and subscribe to the 1-Minute Habits YouTube Channel at www.youtube.com/oneminutehabits.[71]

***

Thank you all so much for your support. I would love to hear about the progress you make and I'm sure others will too. So if you want to, do not hesitate to share it with me, or us through whichever social channel you prefer. By inspiring others you'll give them hope that they can do it as well.

With a strategy like 1-Minute Habits at your disposal, and with a like-minded community there to support you, it will only be a matter of time until you start living a fulfilled life.

References

[1] **New Year's Resolutions Failure Rate:**
http://www.quirkology.com/UK/Experiment_resolution.shtml
&
http://www.statisticbrain.com/new-years-resolution-statistics/

[2] **Planning Fallacy:**
Mark V. Pezzo, Jordan A. Litman, Stephanie P. Pezzo. *On the distinction between yuppies and hippies: Individual differences in prediction biases for planning future tasks.* Personality and Individual Differences 41 (Nov 2006): 1359-1371
http://www.sciencedirect.com/science/article/pii/S019188690600 2194

[3] **How long habits take to form:**
Phillipa L. et al. *How are habits formed: Modelling habit formation in the real world.* European Journal of Social Psychology 40 (Oct 2010): 998-1009
http://onlinelibrary.wiley.com/doi/10.1002/ejsp.674/abstract.

[4] **4 signs of a habit:**
John A.B. *The four horsemen of automaticity: Awareness, Attention, Efficiency, and Control in social cognition.* Handbook of social cognition 1 (1994): 1-40
http://www.unisaarland.de/fak5/excops/download/four_horsem en_of_automaticity.pdf

[5] **Old habits don't die. They hibernate and can be reactivated:**
Ann M.G. *Activity of striatal neurons reflects dynamic encoding and recoding of procedural memories.* Nature 437 (Oct 2005): 1158-61

http://www.nature.com/nature/journal/v437/n7062/abs/nature0
4053.html#a1

[6] Suppressing anxious thoughts doesn't work, and can actually make you more anxious:

Ernst H.W.K. *The paradoxical effects of suppressing anxious thoughts during imminent threat.* Behaviour Research and Therapy 41 (Sep 2003): 1113-20
http://www.ncbi.nlm.nih.gov/pubmed/12914812

[7] Suppressing food cravings may make you dysphoric:

Andrew J.H. *Symposium on 'Molecular mechanisms and psychology of food intake' - The psychology of food craving.* Proceedings of the Nutrition Society 66 (May 2007): 277-85
http://journals.cambridge.org/download.php?file=%2FPNS%2FP
NS66_02%2FS0029665107005502a.pdf&code=b38c4f0e15331e27
3a840b894cced959

[8] Suppressing chocolate cravings can cause over-eating:

Janet P. et al. *The effect of deprivation on food cravings and eating behaviour in restrained and unrestrained eaters.* International Journal of Eating Disorders 38 (Dec 2005): 301-09
http://onlinelibrary.wiley.com/doi/10.1002/eat.20195/abstract

[9] Outside layer is brain's most recent addition:

http://tolweb.org/treehouses/?treehouse_id=3710

[10] Basal Ganglia – main player in habits and automation:

Gregory A.F. et al. *Cortical and basal ganglia contributions to habit learning and automaticity.* Trends in Cognitive Sciences 14 (May 2010): 208-15
http://www.ncbi.nlm.nih.gov/pubmed/20207189

[11] **Damaged Basal Ganglias are associated with many brain disorders:**
http://www.nlm.nih.gov/medlineplus/ency/article/001069.htm

[12] **Many authors indicate fundamental link between personality and Pre-frontal cortex:**
Colin C.G. et al. *Testing predictions from Personality Neuroscience: Brain structure and the Big Five.* Psychological Science 21 (Jun 2010): 820-8
http://www.ncbi.nlm.nih.gov/pmc/articles/PMC3049165/

[13] **Pre-frontal Cortex – The self-control centre of the brain:**
Neural Signature of Self-control:
Marcel B. et al. *To do or not to do: The neural signature of self-control.* The Journal of Neuroscience 22 (Aug 2007): 9141-45
http://www.jneurosci.org/content/27/34/9141.short
Neural link between Intelligence, Self-control, and the Pre-frontal Cortex:
Noah A.S. et al. *Individual differences in Delay Discounting: relation to intelligence, working memory, and anterior prefrontal* cortex. Psychological Science 19 (Sep 2008): 904-11
http://ccpweb.wustl.edu/pdfs/shamosh2008.pdf
Pre-frontal Cortex activity linked with self-control and goal-directed decisions:
Todd A.H. et al. *Self-control in decision-making involves modulation of the vmPFC valuation system.* Science 324 (May 2009): 646-48
http://www.sciencemag.org/content/324/5927/646

[14] **Willpower is a limited resource:**
http://www.apa.org/helpcenter/willpower-limited-resource.pdf

[15] **Roy Baumeister is highly cited:**
http://www.fsu.edu/faculty/fachonors.html#isi

[16] **Experiments showing Willpower is a limited**

resource that diminishes during the day due to Ego-depletion:

Roy F. B. et al. *Ego-depletion: Is the active self a limited resource?* Journal of Personality and Social Psychology 74 (1998): 1252-65

http://www.psychologytoday.com/files/attachments/584/baumeisteretal1998.pdf

[17] More on Willpower and Ego-depletion:

Roy F. B. *Ego-depletion and self-control failure: An energy model of the self's executive function.* Self and Identity 1 (2002): 129-36

http://psych.ut.ee/~nek/isiksus/Baumeister 2002.pdf

[18] The Strength Model of Self-control. Willpower is like a muscle:

Roy F. B. et al. *The Strength Model of Self-control.* Current Directions in Psychological Science 16 (2007): 351-5

http://www.carlsonschool.umn.edu/assets/166733.pdf

[19] Decisions and Choices cause Ego-depletion:

Kathleen D.V. et al. *Making choices impairs subsequent self-control: a limited-resource account of decision-making, self-regulation, and active initiative.* Journal of Personality and Social Psychology 94 (May 2008): 883-98

http://www.ncbi.nlm.nih.gov/pubmed/18444745

[20] Acts of self-control deplete glucose:

Matthew T.G. et al. *Self-control relies on glucose as a limited energy source: Willpower is more than a metaphor.* Journal of Personality and Social Psychology 92 (Feb 2007): 325-36

http://www.uky.edu/~njdewa2/gailliotetal07JPSP.pdf

[21] Increase in glucose can temporarily boost Willpower:

EJ M. et al. *Toward a physiology of dual-process reasoning and judgement: Lemonade, willpower, and expensive rule-based analysis.* Psychological

Science 19 (Mar 2008): 255-60
http://pss.sagepub.com/content/19/3/255

[22] **Too much sugar is bad for you and can make you fat. Who knew?**
http://www.livescience.com/36188-sugar-bad.html

[23] **Decision Fatigue affects judges:**
Shai D. et al. *Extraneous factors in judicial decisions.* Proceedings of the National Academy of Sciences 108 (Apr 2011): 6889
http://www.pnas.org/content/108/17/6889

[24] **Retail outlets take advantage of our impaired cognition:**
Deborah A.C. et al. *Candy at the cash register - A risk factor for obesity and chronic disease.* New England Journal of Medicine 367 (Oct 2012): 1381-83
http://www.nejm.org/doi/full/10.1056/NEJMp1209443

[25] **Meta-analysis on Ego-depletion. Willpower is a Limited Resource, and it has 5 prevalent causes:**
Martin S.H. et al. *Ego-depletion and the strength model of self-control: A meta-analysis.* Psychological Bulletin (American Psychological Association) 136 (Jul 2010): 495-525
http://www.ncbi.nlm.nih.gov/pubmed/20565167

[26] **If you want to change the world, don't focus on changing the world. Focus on Small Wins.**
Karl E.W. *Small wins: Redefining the scale of social problems.* American Psychologist 39 (Jan 1984): 40-9
http://redhooksummit.com/wpcontent/uploads/2013/06/Small-Wins-article.pdf

[27] **Our energy-conserving brain makes our muscles feel more tired than they really are:**

Timothy D.N. et al. *Evidence that a central governor regulates exercise performance during acute hypoxia and hyperoxia.* The Journal of Experimental Biology 204 (Sep 2001): 3225-34
http://jeb.biologists.org/content/204/18/3225.full

[28] By focusing on our limited willpower, we may actually convince ourselves that we have less energy than we really do:

Veronika J. et al. *Ego-depletion - Is it all in your head? Implicity theories about willpower affect self-regulation.* Psychological Science 21 (Nov 2010): 1686-93
http://pss.sagepub.com/content/21/11/1686

[29] We are Negatively Biased:

Roy F.B. et al. *Bad is stronger than good.* Review of General Psychology 5 (2001): 323-70
http://www.carlsonschool.umn.edu/assets/71516.pdf

[30] Lack of Willpower is the main cause of failing to reach goals, according to American Psychological Association Survey:

http://www.apa.org/news/press/releases/2012/02/willpower.aspx

[31] Willpower correlates with health, happiness, and success:

June P.T. et al. *High self-control predicts good adjustment, less pathology, better grades, and interpersonal success.* The Journal of Personality 72 (Apr 2004): 271-324
http://www.ncbi.nlm.nih.gov/pubmed/15016066

[32] Meta-analysis on self-control and longevity of life. More self-control = Longer life:

Margaret L.K. et al. *Do conscientious individuals live longer? A quantitative review.* Health Psychology 27 (Sep 2008): 505-12 http://www.ncbi.nlm.nih.gov/pubmed/18823176

[33] **Willpower predicts grades better than IQ:**
Angela L.D. et al. *Self-discipline outdoes IQ in predicting academic performance of adolescents.* Psychological Science 16 (Dec 2005): 939-44
http://pss.sagepub.com/content/16/12/939.short

[34] **32 year study showing that willpower predicts how well your life may turn out:**
Terrie E.M. et al. *A gradient of childhood self-control predicts health, wealth, and public safety.* Proceedings from the National Academy of Sciences 108 (Feb 2011): 2693-98
http://www.pnas.org/content/108/7/2693.long

[35] **Jerry Seinfeld is the richest Actor and Comedian in the World:**
http://www.wealthx.com/articles/2014/comedian-jerry-seinfeld-tops-wealth-xs-hollywood-and-bollywood-rich-list/

[36] **Jerry Seinfeld's 'Don't Break the Chain' method:**
http://lifehacker.com/281626/jerry-seinfelds-productivity-secret

[37] **Print free calendars for Chains Tracking:**
http://www.printfree.com/Calendars.htm

[38] **Visually appealing Chains Tracking website:**
https://chains.cc/

[39] **Writing things down makes them easier to remember:**
Pablo B. et al. *Treating thoughts as material objects can increase or decrease their impact on evaluation.* Psychological Science 24 (Jan 2013): 41-7
http://pss.sagepub.com/content/24/1/41.full.pdf+html?ijkey=UUa5dZpd6DaeE&keytype=ref&siteid=sppss

[40] Trivial uncomfortable actions strengthen Willpower:
Roy F.B. et al. *Self-regulation and personality: How interventions increase regulatory success, and how depletion moderates the effects of traits on behaviour.* The Journal of Personality 74 (Dec 2006): 1773-801
http://www.uky.edu/~njdewa2/baumeisteretaljpers06.pdf
&
Megan O. et al. *Improvements in self-control from financial monitoring.* The Journal of Economic Psychology 28 (Aug 2007): 487-501
http://www.sciencedirect.com/science/article/pii/S016748700600
1012

[41] Stress hinders the Pre-frontal Cortex and makes us more impulsive:
Amy F.T.A. *Stress signalling pathways that impair pre-frontal cortex structure and function.* Nature Reviews Neuroscience 10 (Jun 2009): 410-22
http://www.nature.com/nrn/journal/v10/n6/execsumm/nrn264
8.html

[42] Too much stress harms the mind and body, and can lead to serious illnesses:
http://www.apa.org/helpcenter/stress.aspx

[43] High Heart Rate Variability promotes Self-control:
Julian F.T. et al. *Heart rate variability, prefrontal neural function, and cognitive performance: The neurovisceral integration perspective on self-regulation, adaptation, and health.* Annals of Behaviour Medicine 37 (Apr 2009): 141-53
http://link.springer.com/article/10.1007%2Fs12160-009-9101-z

[44] Health degeneration, and illness reduces Heart Rate Variability:
Lise S.N. et al. *Self-regulatory deficits in fibromyalgia and temporomandibular disorders.* Pain 151 (Oct 2010): 37-44

http://www.painjournalonline.com/article/S0304-3959(10)00293-9/abstract

[45] Meta-analysis on Meditation:
Peter S. et al. *The psychological effects of Meditation: A meta-analysis.* Psychological Bulletin 138 (Nov 2012): 1139-71
http://psycnet.apa.org/index.cfm?fa=buy.optionToBuy&id=2012-12792-001

[46] Meditation reshapes our brain and makes them thicker in some areas:
Sara W.L. et al. *Meditation experience is associated with increased cortical thickness.* Neuroreport 16 (Nov 2005): 1893-7
http://www.ncbi.nlm.nih.gov/pmc/articles/PMC1361002/
&
TEDx Talk on Meditation reshaping the brain:
http://www.youtube.com/watch?v=m8rRzTtP7Tc

[47] Meditation increases Heart Rate Variability:
Caroline P. et al. *Heart rate dynamics in different levels of Zen Meditation.* International Journal of Cardiology 145 (Nov 2010): 142-6
http://www.ncbi.nlm.nih.gov/pubmed/19631997

[48] Meta-analyses on Exercise Benefits:
Chad D.R. et al. *The antidepressive effects of exercise: A meta-analysis of randomised trials.* Sports Medicine 39 (2009): 491-511
http://www.ncbi.nlm.nih.gov/pubmed/19453207
&
Matthew P.H. et al. *Effect of exercise training on depressive symptoms among patients with a chronic illness: A systematic review and meta-analysis of randomised controlled trials.* Archives of Internal Medicine 172 (Jan 2012): 101-11
http://archinte.jamanetwork.com/article.aspx?articleid=1108677

[49] Exercise makes your brain bigger:

Stanley J.C. et al. *Aerobic exercise training increases brain volume in aging humans.* The Journals of Gerontology: Series A, Biological Sciences and Medical Sciences 61 (Nov 2006): 1166-70
http://www2.pitt.edu/~bachlab/LabSite/Publications.html/colco mbe2006.pdf

[50] Exercise increases Heart Rate Variability:
Anita L.H. et al. *Heart rate variability and its relation to prefrontal cognitive function: The effects of training and detraining.* European Journal of Applied Psychology 93 (Dec 2004): 263-72
http://link.springer.com/article/10.1007/s00421-004-1208-0

[51] Exercise makes you more attentive and reduces chocolate cravings:
Adrian H.T. et al. *Acute effects of brisk walking on urges to eat chocolate, affect, and responses to a stressor and chocolate cue. An experimental study.* Appetite 52 (Feb 2009): 155-60
http://www.ncbi.nlm.nih.gov/pubmed/18835411

[52] Meta-analysis on how much Green Exercise you should do:
Jo B. et al. *What is the best dose of nature and green exercise for improving mental health? A multi-study analysis.* Environmental Science and Technology 44 (May 2010): 3947-55
http://www.julespretty.com/wp-content/uploads/2013/09/4.-Dose-of-Nature-EST-Barton-Pretty-May-2010.pdf

[53] Sleep deprivation amplifies your response to negative stimuli, making you stressed and cranky:
Seung-Schik Y. et al. *The human emotional brain without sleep - A prefrontal amygdala disconnect.* Current Biology 17 (Oct 2007): R877-78
http://walkerlab.berkeley.edu/reprints/Yoo-Walker_CurrBiol_2007.pdf

[54] Meta-analyses on Sleep deprivation:

June J.P. et al. *Effects of sleep deprivation on performance: a meta-analysis.* Sleep 19 (May 1996): 318-26
http://www.ncbi.nlm.nih.gov/pubmed/8776790

    &

    Julian L. et al. *A meta-analysis of the impact of short-term sleep deprivation on cognitive variables.* Psychological Bulletin 136 (May 2010): 375-89
https://www.med.upenn.edu/uep/user_documents/Lim2010-Ameta-analysisoftheimpactofshort-termsleepdeprivationoncognitivevariables..pdf

[55] Sleep deprivation makes your Pre-frontal Cortex mildly dysfunctional:

William D.S.K. et al. *Sleep deprivation reduces perceived emotional intelligence and constructive thinking skills.* Sleep Medicine 9 (Jul 2008): 517-26
http://www.ncbi.nlm.nih.gov/pubmed/17765011

[56] Sleep deprivation puts you in a similar state of a mildly drunk person:

David E. et al. *Performance impairment during four days partial sleep deprivation compared with the acute effects of alcohol and hypoxia.* Sleep Medicine 10 (Feb 2009): 189-97
http://www.ncbi.nlm.nih.gov/pubmed/18276188

[57] A good night's sleep can return brain function to an optimal level.

Stanley J.C. et al. *Aerobic exercise training increases brain volume in aging humans.* The Journals of Gerontology: Series A, Biological Sciences and Medical Sciences 61 (Nov 2006): 1166-70
http://www.ncbi.nlm.nih.gov/pubmed/18788652

[58] Deep, slow breathing increases Heart Rate Variability:

Hye-Sue S. et al. *The effects of specific respiratory rates on heart rate and*

heart rate variability. Applied Psychophysiology and Biofeedback 28 (Mar 2003): 13-23
https://www.depts.ttu.edu/hess/mccomb/documents/hrv_article s/Specific Respiratory Rates and HRV.pdf)

[59] **Being bad at Meditation is still beneficial for you. Distracted Meditation helps your focus outside Meditations:**
Yi-Yuan T. et al. *Short-term meditation induces white matter changes in the anterior cingulate.* Proceedings of the National Academy of Sciences 107 (Aug 2010): 15649-52
http://www.pnas.org/content/107/35/15649.full.pdf
    &
    Britta K.H. et al. *Mindfulness practice leads to increases in regional brain gray matter density.* Psychiatry Research 191 (Jan 2011): 36-43
http://www.ncbi.nlm.nih.gov/pubmed/21071182

[60] **Mess makes you stressed. Cleaning can be good for your mind and health:**
Darby E.S. et al. *No Place Like Home: Home Tours Correlate With Daily Patterns of Mood and Cortisol.* Personality and Social Psychology Bulletin 36 (Jan 2010): 71-81
http://undecidedthebook.files.wordpress.com/2012/07/saxbe-repetti-pspb-2010.pdf

[61] **Positive Affects replenish Willpower:**
Roy F. B. *Ego-depletion and self-control failure: An energy model of the self's executive function.* Self and Identity 1 (2002): 129-36
http://psych.ut.ee/~nek/isiksus/Baumeister 2002.pdf.

[62] **Being happy makes you smile. But smiling can also make you happy:**
Tara L.K. et al. *Grin and bear it: The influence of manipulated facial expression on the stress response.* Psychological Science 23 (Nov 2012): 1372-8
http://www.scribd.com/doc/119200793/Grin-and-Bear-It-The-

Influence-of-Manipulated-Facial-Expression-on-the-Stress-Response

[63] **Many studies show that forced laughing has a lot of benefits, such as improving health and mood:**
http://www.bupa.co.uk/individuals/health-information/health-news-index/2005/hi-160305-laugh

[64] **1-Minute of Forced Laughter can make you more positive and happy.**
Erin F. et al. *Effect of forced laughter on mood.* Psychological Reports 90 (Feb 2002): 184
http://www.ncbi.nlm.nih.gov/pubmed/11898980

[65] **We overestimate our willpower:**
Loran F.N. et al. *The restraint bias: how the illusion of self-restraint promotes impulsive behaviour.* Psychological Science 20 (Dec 2009): 1523-8
http://www.ncbi.nlm.nih.gov/pubmed/19883487

[66] **Review 1-Minute Habits on Amazon (sign in to verify):**
http://amzn.to/1olR06x

[67] **1-Minute Habits Facebook:**
facebook.com/oneminutehabits

[68] **My Blog on Optimising Life:**
raghibahmed.com

[69] **1-Minute Habits Twitter:**
twitter.com/oneminutehabits

[70] **1-Minute Habits Pinterest:**
pinterest.com/oneminutehabits

[71] **1-Minute Habits YouTube Channel:**
youtube.com/oneminutehabits

CPSIA information can be obtained at www.ICGtesting.com
Printed in the USA
LVOW01s1722180615

442986LV00025B/744/P

9 781503 009820